Duncan Bannatyne is one of Britain's best known entrepreneurs, thanks to his appearances on *Dragon's Den*. A regular investor in new companies, he is chairman of the Bannatyne Group, which owns and operates hotels, health clubs, bars and restaurants. In 2009, the *Sunday Times* Rich List estimated his personal worth at £320 million, but he started his business career with an investment of £450 in an ice-cream van.

His first book, *Anyone Can Do It*, was a *Sunday Times* bestseller in both hardback and paperback and has sold 200,000 copies. He has six children, and homes in London, the North East and Cannes.

His website is at **www.bannatyne.co.uk**

Jo Monroe, who worked with Duncan Bannatyne on the writing of this book, is a journalist who has written for *The Times*, the *Guardian*, the *Observer* and *Time Out*.

Her website is at **www.professionalghost.com**

How To Be Smart With Your Money

DUNCAN BANNATYNE

An Orion paperback

First published in Great Britain in 2009
by Orion
This paperback edition published in 2010
by Orion Books Ltd,
Orion House, 5 Upper St Martin's Lane,
London WC2H 9EA

An Hachette UK company

10 9 8 7 6 5 4 3 2 1

A CIP catalogue record for this book
is available from the British Library.

ISBN 978-1-4091-1713-1

Printed and bound in Great Britain by Clays Ltd, St Ives plc

The Orion Publishing Group's policy is to use papers that
are natural, renewable and recyclable products and
made from wood grown in sustainable forests. The logging
and manufacturing processes are expected to conform to
the environmental regulations of the country of origin.

www.orionbooks.co.uk

Contents

TO MY CHILDREN

Abigail, Hollie, Jennifer, Eve, Emily and Tom

Remember I love you more...

Acknowledgements

First and foremost I would like to thank my beautiful wife, Joanne, and my children, Abigail, Hollie, Jennifer, Eve, Emily, Tom and not forgetting my grandchild Ava. Thank you and I love you all so much.

I would like to thank Jo Monroe for working with me a third time; it has been an absolute pleasure. Thanks also to Alan Samson at the Orion Publishing Group and Jonny Geller at Curtis Brown; your help with this book has been invaluable.

A big thank you to everyone.

Introduction

Some people just seem to be smart with money, while others let it slip through their fingers as soon as they get it. I believe there are strategies and tactics that can not only help us to be smarter with money, but also let us build a more secure future for ourselves. These ideas work whether we're in a boom or a bust and, over a lifetime, can bring real benefits to anyone who gets to grips with them.

Being smart with money isn't difficult; it simply requires you to look carefully at your finances and make responsible decisions. Being smart with money isn't about having lots of it – it's just about making the most of what you've got. Whether your income is from state benefits or a trust fund, I firmly believe that it's not just how much money you have, but what you do with it that makes the difference.

In Britain, we have an odd way of talking about money. We'll brag about how much or how little we paid for our car, but we won't talk about how much we earn. It's as if it's a taboo subject – even some married couples don't discuss their salaries or their spending habits (which is probably why money problems are cited as the second-biggest cause of divorce after infidelity). We have experts on TV telling us how we can save £30 on our gas bill or our home insurance, but not how we can save for our futures. As the old saying goes, we know the price of everything and the value of nothing.

It doesn't help that we have become distant from money. I remember getting my weekly wages – in cash – in a small brown envelope with details of deductions written on it. I could touch it, feel it and count it, but now our income bypasses us and goes straight into our bank accounts. We don't spend cash any more so we no longer see the amount from our wage packets reducing, which makes it harder to count how much we've got left.

I believe there are some basic skills we can all acquire that enable us to have a much better relationship with money. Being good with money is not that hard, yet it's an area of our lives that we often defer to 'experts' because it seems so complicated. These days, children get taught a little about money at school, but most of us have never had any education about how to look after it. So it's no wonder that so many people get into bad money habits or get caught in a cycle of debt. And I'm not just talking about people on the breadline here – one of the biggest lessons of the credit crunch has been that many people working in our financial institutions didn't understand the fundamental rules of being good with money. If there was a GCSE in Money, then perhaps we'd all be better off.

I want to explain how money works: if you know what controls money, you can make smarter decisions about what you do with it. As the fallout from the financial turmoil that started in 2007 continues to impact on all our lives, I think it has become blindingly obvious that if we don't *understand* money, then it's going to control us rather than the other way around.

Boom and bust

When I started work on this book, people said to me that it must be a nightmare to write because I'd surely have to change my advice depending on the latest catastrophic headline. While it certainly might have been easier to write this kind of book in the mid-1990s when jobs were easier to find, stocks pretty much always went up and property soared in value, writing this book in turbulent times has helped me focus on what really matters with money management. In chaotic times it's not possible to say 'take out a pension', 'get a better paying job' or 'get into buy-to-let' because it's clear that the financial certainties of the past couple of decades have not been certainties at all.

So what I've tried to do with this book is to return to the fundamentals of money, to pass on the essential rules that guide its ebb and flow so that you can make the best decisions about your financial well-being. I'm not going to tell you whether or not you should take out a pension or use up your ISA allowance; I'm going to give you the information so that *you* can decide if it's right for you. That way, this book should stand the test of time – these are universal rules and the advice here holds true if we're in a recession or a boom. I have no axe to grind, no product or philosophy to promote. I don't mind if you follow my advice, I only care that you've got enough information to know which bits of advice are right for you and which bits aren't.

If the recent financial turmoil has taught us anything, it's that we can't live beyond our means for long. The mistakes of bankers and individuals who borrowed more than they knew they would ever be able to repay have proved to me that we all need to be responsible. Money is too important, too fundamental to 21st-century life, to leave to 'experts' to sort out. We need to be responsible for our own financial choices, and it's my hope that this book will give you the confidence to take the reins of your finances.

The sooner you start, the better

What has become clear as I've written this book is that the sooner you take control of your finances the better and, frankly, that sometimes means the younger you are, the better. The long-term returns that pensions, savings, property and stock-market investments offer are much greater if you have the luxury of time to ride out a couple of financial storms. If you can avoid debt in your twenties and get an early start on the housing ladder, your long-term financial future will look bright. However, I got to my 30th birthday with barely a penny to my name so I know it's possible to make up for lost time. I know others who left it to their forties before they found financial security. Even if you are nearing retirement, there are tools and suggestions here that will have an immediate effect on your finances if you take them on board.

I completely understand why so many of us drift through life without taking our finances in hand; it doesn't help that the TV news is full of arbitrary statistics, interest rates, exchange rates, inflation rates, share prices and jargon that baffle and bamboozle us – how do these things actually affect us? No one ever says! And when we do talk to the people who should know about money – our bank managers and financial advisers – we don't get advice, just a sales pitch for a new financial 'product' or 'vehicle'. Sometimes it seems that financial services are deliberately made complicated so that we won't understand them and won't be able to shop around for a better deal! We find it impossible to take control of our finances because we're just not given the skills or the information we need.

Worrying about money blights many people's lives. Will we have enough to pay the bills? Will we ever earn enough to clear our debts? What will happen if we can't meet the final demands or pay for the school trip? We tie ourselves up in knots about money and in the end it gets so complicated – and so depressing – that the only way to cope is to ignore it. And when that happens, things will only get worse.

And if we're not worrying about money, we're dreaming about it – about the cars and houses we'd like to buy. The problem I see is that between *worrying* about money, and *dreaming* about it, so many of us forget to *think* about it. A lot of the advice in this book encourages you to start thinking about money in a practical way and move you away from useless panicking and unhelpful dreaming.

My life has taught me about the importance of money: I know what it's like not to have it, and I know what it's like to be wealthy and – crucially – I know how hard you have to work to earn it. I was born into an extremely poor family where there was never any money around. The only time I had any as a kid was when I got a paper round so I could save up for a bicycle. For 15 years after I left school, I drifted from one dead-end job to another, sometimes saving up enough to buy a car, sometimes having to sell the car because I'd run out of cash. It wasn't until my thirties that I started a business and set out on the road to becoming wealthy. My journey has taught me to *value* money rather than *count* it.

This book isn't about getting rich, it's about taking control. By the end of it, you'll have the confidence to make decisions that are right for you and the skills to make your money go further and work harder for you – no matter what happens to the economy.

What's in this book?

This isn't a book about cutting out coupons or the best way to reduce your household bills – there are other books on the shelves about living frugally and websites where you can compare prices. This book isn't about the edges of your financial life where you can save a tenner there or get an extra 5% here: it's about the fundamentals of finance and your core relationship with money.

This book isn't about global economics either, nor will it give you specific advice about financial products that will be out of date by the time it hits the shelves. I won't be able to give you answers to specific concerns or problems, but I *can* give you information that will let you work out your own answers. This book is about understanding long-term, fundamental principles and behaviour that will enable you to be in charge of your financial options. I'm going to introduce you to some basic theories about money and show how balancing five factors – earning, spending, borrowing, saving and investing – is the key to financial security.

Over the years, I've developed a series of concepts that have really helped me to understand money and enabled me to make the most of whatever I've had. For me, being good with money means insulating oneself from the worst the financial world has to throw at us and making the most of the economic opportunities that come along. This book will show you how.

The book has three parts to it. A bit like learning to drive, Part One is the theory section where I'm going to share some of my observations about what money is and how it's controlled. The next section of the book contains the practical sections where I'll discuss strategies and options for the major factors that influence our financial lives. And then, finally, instead of taking a driving test, I'm going to take you through the preparation of your own personal financial plan.

You don't have to read the book in the sequence it's been laid out. For example, if you want to start with the section on saving, then go ahead. It might even be that some of the theoretical stuff in Part One will sink in a bit better once you've read the practical stuff in Part Two. It's my hope that no matter what order you read the book in, when you take it as a whole they add up to a comprehensive guide to understanding money that will enable you to take responsibility for your financial choices and that will ultimately make you wealthier.

Who's this book for?

You don't have to know any jargon to be able to get the most out of this book (I've tried to avoid it as much as possible and added a glossary of financial terms at the back just in case). You don't have to have money in the bank or a good credit rating. You don't even have to know what a 'credit rating' is or why it's important. Whether you've got money in the bank or not, whether you're 18 or 80, self-employed, unemployed, or working 9 to 5, the principles of being smart with your money are the same. So if you want to make the most of what you've got, this book is for you.

My history with money

I grew up as one of seven children in a council house in Clydebank. My dad worked in the local factory and money was extremely tight. When the ice-cream van came round I was told I couldn't have one because 'we were poor'. The only time I had money was when I got a paper round so I could save up to buy a bike and my ambition was to be 'not poor'.

I worked as a stoker in the Royal Navy and earned so little that I didn't need a bank account. When I was dishonourably discharged (for throwing my commanding officer overboard!), I was nineteen and had no qualifications or prospects.

I spent my twenties is a series of dead-end jobs – cabbying, bar work, working in garages, selling ice-creams on the beach – and spent every penny I earned. As I approached 30, I realised that my party lifestyle couldn't continue as I wanted to settle down and start a family. I made the decision to turn my life around and made a promise to myself and my soon-to-be wife that I would become a millionaire.

I finally got a bank account when I was 30 so I could stockpile the cash I was saving towards a deposit for a house while working shifts in a bakery. I made extra money on the side doing up cars I'd bought at auction. When an ice-cream van came up for auction I bought it for £450 and started an ice-cream business. Within a few years I had a fleet of six vans, lucrative concessions in local parks and a turnover of £300,000 a year. I used some of the cash to buy up cheap property that I rented to Social Security tenants.

1986–1997

I sold the ice-cream business, my car and even my house to start my next business, Quality Care Homes. We offered superior elderly care in purpose-built residential homes and when I ran out of cash building the first home, I borrowed £30,000 on credit cards to complete the project. I expanded to nine homes and floated the company on the stock exchange for £18 million. I continued to expand, and sold my share of the business in 1997 for £46 million. During this time I also started other ventures, including children's day care nurseries and health clubs.

1997–present

Bannatyne's is now the largest privately owned health club chain in the country with 180,000 members in 60 clubs. In 2004 my personal wealth was estimated by the *Sunday Times* rich list to be £100 million. In 2008, they calculated my net worth to be £310 million.

PART ONE

The theory of money

1.
Money is a tool – you've got to learn how to use it

Have you ever stopped to think about what money actually is? If that sounds like a weird question, take a look at a bank note. That £5 note isn't actually five pounds: if you look carefully you'll see the words 'I promise to pay the bearer on demand the sum of five pounds'. What that means is that your £5 note is just a promise of five pounds.

When I was a kid I thought that meant that I could knock on the door of the Bank of Scotland and exchange my note for five actual pounds, which I've always presumed would be made of gold. I've no idea what would happen if you actually tried to do that, but I'd be willing to bet that you'd probably get some strange looks and be asked to move along! And if we all turned up and asked for our 'pounds' in exchange for our notes, I don't suppose there would be enough gold to go round.

So if money isn't a real thing, if it's nothing more than a promise for something you can't get your hands on, what is it? Over the years I've heard lots of explanations about money being 'a unit of exchange' – something that can be exchanged for something else of equal value – or even an 'illusion' because money only works if we believe that your £5 note is worth whatever you buy with it. I can't quite get my head round those explanations, but I get that the key point is that money isn't actually very valuable in itself, it's only when we *do* something with it that it has a value.

Personally, I see money as a tool. And like a hammer, it's only really worth something if you use it. Sure, it's great to have a hammer in your shed in case you need one, but it's only really of value when it helps you drive a nail into a wall or a stake into the ground. A hammer is a tool that can help you achieve a certain outcome, and money is no different.

Now you might well be able to drive a stake into the ground with your bare hands, but the hammer makes it a lot easier. And of course, if you can afford a bigger hammer, the job gets even easier. Let's make no mistake – things get easier when you have more money, but the key thing here is that it's still *you* doing the hammering, it's still *your* muscle power, *your* brain deciding what to hammer. Without you and your know-how, the hammer is pretty much useless. So the key to being smart with money is not just to have more of it, but to use what you've got more wisely.

You might think that a pound on its own can't do very much (unless you buy a winning lottery ticket with it, of course), but if you don't fritter your small change away and save it instead, you build up a lump sum. The more money you have, the more powerful a tool it becomes and the more you can do with it. If you don't have a pound to spare, don't worry, later in the book there are a lot of suggestions for ways to get your hands on extra cash.

If you can create a bit of financial muscle by gathering together your individual pounds into a lump sum, imagine how much power we create if we join our lump sums together. The best example I can think of is giving to charity. If we all give £5 to thousands of different causes, it doesn't help very much, but if we co-ordinate our donations and all give our £5 to an organisation like Sport Relief, suddenly there's a huge total that can be powerful enough to create real change. I've been on trips with Sport Relief to Ethiopia and seen just what a force for change money can be – and it can bring some pretty incredible changes in your life too.

The same force for change is created when we deposit money with a bank. The banks can then lend all our tiny bits of savings to individuals and companies that can make more money, some of which is returned to us in interest payments. Another example is starting a business: you might not be able to afford to start a business on your own, but with a few friends, you might have the capital to launch a new venture. The stock markets make this even easier: you probably can't afford to buy a whole company on your own, but you can buy a few shares that will hopefully increase in value as the company uses the muscle power of all that lumped-together money. So even if you don't have very much of your own, you can join your money together with other people's small amounts to create a really valuable tool.

The flow of money

The fact is that we are all connected by money. A very basic illustration is the £5 note that I receive in change in one shop and spend in another, which ends up in your wallet. Money flows between us, which means that what one person does affects another. This is why when US banks started lending recklessly to people who could never be expected to repay their home loans, the phrase 'sub-prime mortgage lending' became headline news all over the world because our financial lives are so interconnected.

The recent past has shown clearly how one person's financial choice affects another person's bank balance. When banks started to fail in America in September 2008, investors lost confidence in British banks too and sold their shares, which sent share prices down. Shares in HBOS, the Halifax Bank of Scotland group, lost 90% of their value. In turn, this meant anyone holding shares in HBOS had lost a lot of money and savers with money in the Halifax became very nervous. Yet while fortunes were being lost, there were also quite a few people making money and that's because they understood something fundamental about the nature of money . . .

Just like the basic physics of water, the flow of money between us creates a force. Just as a stream can be harnessed to turn a watermill, understanding the flow of money can enable you to harness the power of money. This is why I say that it doesn't necessarily matter how much money you have: if you can get close enough to the stream you can start to benefit, and a lot of this book will be about helping you identify the flow of money.

The first key to being smart with money is to stop seeing it as a finite thing in itself and start thinking about it as a device that can be leveraged to your own advantage. Money is not an end in itself, but it does give you the means to get there.

 **CHECKLIST**

✔ **Money is a tool that can help you create change.**

✔ **The more money you have, the more power you have to create change.**

✔ **Money connects us: what happens in one part of the economy has an effect elsewhere.**

2.
Stop worrying, stop dreaming – start *thinking*

Even **really smart people** aren't always smart with money. For some reason, it's a subject huge numbers of people just can't handle and if they tell themselves that 'they're just not very good with money' then they can let themselves off the hook for not getting on top of their finances. When the subject of money comes up, there's a big percentage of people who just put their fingers in their ears and choose not to listen. From what I can tell, they've decided that money is far more complicated than it really is and, as they'll never understand it, they may as well just switch off.

This is rubbish. The rules that govern money are pretty straightforward and all you have to do is engage with the subject a little bit, and things that once sounded bizarre will start to make sense. So my only absolute rule of being smart about money is to THINK about it.

When there are bills to pay, kids to feed, debts to repay, you just don't get a chance to think about money because every penny is spent before you even get your hands on it. It passes through your fingers within seconds so you never get a chance to think about what you want to do with it. It's so easy to go through life worrying about money instead of really thinking about it, but if you make the switch from worrying to thinking, you'll be on the right road.

The fact that you've picked up this book and made it this far tells me you want to be better with money, and if you've found enough time to read the first few pages, then you can create enough time in your life to think about money. If the only thing you get out of this book is a few hours spent thinking about your financial life rather than ignoring it, then this will be the most valuable book you've ever read.

When I say 'thinking' about money, let's be absolutely clear that I don't mean daydreaming! I'm not asking you to think about what you'd buy if you won the lottery, I'm asking you to think about some pretty basic things:

- How much do you have?
- How much do you need?
- Where can you get a bit more from?
- How can you manage what you've got a bit better?

So let's start with a really simple question: how much money do you have in the bank? It's a straightforward enough question but it's amazing how many people can't answer it. If you don't know the answer, how do you know if you can afford that last pint in the pub or that treat you've been promising yourself? You might be able to take cash out to pay for those things, but *paying* for them and *affording* them are two very different concepts.

Here's another simple question: how much money do you need to live on each month? If you can't answer that question, then how can you possibly know if you're earning enough to cover your costs? And if you suspect that you're ending up in the red, if you're smart with money you'll already be asking yourself the next question: where can I get a bit more from?

If you haven't been asking these questions, and you've just been paying the bills as they come in without thinking about them as long as your bank will give you the money, then I reckon you fit into one of two very different camps: you're either really rich or you're more broke than you realise.

If you've sensed for a while that your financial life is a bit of a mess, I completely understand why you haven't asked yourself these basic questions – it's because you're scared of the answers. It's my hope that by the time you finish this book, those answers won't hold any fear for you: if you are in the red and panicking, you need to know that the first step of sorting your finances out is by calculating what your current financial position is. The next chapter is all about that.

Once you've got a grasp of your basic financial situation, you need to keep thinking about money.

- Am I earning enough?
- Am I borrowing at the lowest rates?
- What are my priorities for the next week/month/year?
- What extra expense am I likely to incur in the near future?

We'll cover all of this in detail later on, but right now I just want you to start thinking financially. Take the first question in the list: you might think it's a joke question – the answer is always 'no', right? – but it's actually really important. Getting hold of money isn't easy, and if you're wasting your career in a job that isn't rewarding you financially, then it's time to look for another one. If you've been in the same company for years, the chances are your pay rises haven't kept pace with the salaries new recruits are asking for at interviews. You need to start looking at every area of your financial life and think about whether you're earning enough or paying too much.

Learning to prioritise is an essential financial tool. If you spend money on the wrong things, you might not have enough left over for the things you really need. If you spend everything you earn every month, you're never going to be able to save or invest for your future. It can be very difficult to see beyond the end of the month, but I want you to be able to see even further into the future so that you can make plans. Not all of our money fits into the monthly and weekly cycle of salaries and wages: whether it's a holiday, a splurge in the garden centre at the beginning of summer or increased use of the central heating over winter, there are peaks and troughs in our spending. If you can anticipate when this extra expenditure will be required, you can budget for it.

As well as these day-to-day and month-to-month decisions,

I also want you to think about a handful of really big questions:

- Where do you want to be in a year's time?
- What will your life be like in five years' time?
- What kind of lifestyle do you aspire to?
- What kind of retirement would you like to enjoy?

If the questions you've already asked yourself are about coping in the short term, these bigger questions are about succeeding in the long term. I'm going to let you into a secret: it's the foundation of why I became wealthy. It's dead simple: I made the *decision* to become wealthy. I also started a series of businesses and worked extremely hard, but that followed on from my initial decision to take control of my life.

I was just coming up to 30 and I wanted to get married and have kids. I knew I wanted my children to have the things my parents hadn't been able to buy for me. I knew I wanted them to grow up in a nice house – and I knew there was no way I could afford that kind of lifestyle. I made the decision to become wealthy. I started by working every shift I could at a local bakery to save up the deposit so we could buy a house. Then I did that house up so I could sell it for a profit. I made money on the side doing up second-hand cars – whatever it took to take me from penniless to secure. I had a vision of the life I wanted to lead, and that vision guided the choices I made in my early thirties. When I saw the opportunity to start a business, I started to see a completely different future for me and my new family.

A lot has been written about how visualising something can help make it happen (if you ever read a book on sales techniques, it will tell you to imagine making the sale before you talk to a potential customer because *seeing* how a sales pitch can turn out right is the key to *making* it turn out right) and although it sounds a bit far-fetched, I think it's absolutely true. Imagining the kind of life you want is the first step to getting there. If you know what you want, then you can plan for it, aim for it and budget for it. Knowing what you want out of life makes it much easier to prioritise the things you spend your money on. And getting what you want out of life is really what being smart with money is all about.

If you don't think strategically about money, you won't be able to do anything strategic with the money that passes through your bank account and your wallet. I know it sounds a little bit crazy, but thinking about money really is the foundation of getting the most out of it.

CHECKLIST

✔ Worrying about money, or dreaming about it, is not the same as thinking about it.

✔ Think about what you want to do with your money before you get it, that way you won't waste it.

✔ Planning your financial future is the first step towards making it a reality.

3.
Budgeting is rewarding

If there is one basic, fundamental, unchanging way of being smart with money it is this: you've got to have more coming in than you've got going out. And the way to make sure that this happens is by learning to prepare and control your personal budget.

You don't have to be a whizz with a spreadsheet, you don't have to go out and buy a ledger book from the stationers, you don't even have to be very good at maths (as long as you know how to use a calculator): you just have to have a bit of common sense – and a pen and a piece of paper.

Most people earn money monthly and pay for things like rent and bills monthly, so for this exercise I'm going to talk about monthly totals. However, you may not be on a regular salary, you might get paid in lump sums throughout the year, or pay for your rent and bills weekly or by topping-up when you need to. If working out monthly totals isn't relevant to you, then do this exercise in exactly the same way, but calculate either your weekly or annual totals. The important thing is that you stick to one measure and don't mix up your monthly income with your weekly outgoings.

Preparing your budget is easy – you just need to know what your income and your outgoings are.

Income

Write down your monthly net income i.e. your earnings after tax and National Insurance Contributions (NICs) have been deducted. Now think about all your other sources of income – tax credits, child support payments, benefits, maybe interest on savings, anything and everything you can think of. You might have tax to pay on some of those additional income streams, so set aside any tax payable to come up with the net figure. What you want to find out here is how much money you have coming in to spend each month.

	Amount
Net salary	£
Tax credits	£
Benefits	£
Interest on savings	£
Second job	£
Other	£
Total	£

Outgoings

Now list everything you pay for each month: from mortgage payments to bank charges to the newspaper you buy on the way to the station. It can be really difficult to remember everything we pay for, so the best thing is probably to dig out your past three bank statements so that you include all your direct debits, standing orders, loan repayments and regular transfers. Instead of writing down every newspaper you've bought, you could just tot up all the cash you've taken out. Take an average figure from the three statements to come up with a reasonably accurate monthly figure.

	Amount
Rent/mortgage	£
Electricity	£
Gas	£
Phone	£
Council tax	£
Mobile phone	£
Broadband	£
Food	£
Travel	£
Car	£
TV subscription	£
Gym membership	£
Going out	£
Loan repayments	£
Other	£
Total	£

Simple sums

Pretty obviously, the thing to do now is to see if your income is greater than your outgoings. The purpose of a budget is to make sure that you have enough money to pay for the things you need each month. If you've calculated that you break even each month, that's great. If you've found out that you have a few quid over at the end of the month, your budget can also tell you that you can afford to put some extra into savings or investments. And if you end each month short, your budget can help you decide where you can cut back on your expenditure.

If you always have a fairly good idea of your income and expenditure, then it should always be pretty easy to determine if you can afford whatever it is you're thinking about buying – which is why balancing your budget is one of the fundamental skills of good money management.

Adjusting your budget

Let me ask you a question: how does your budget make you feel? Are you relieved? Surprised? Concerned? I want you to have a budget that you are happy with and this may mean playing around with some of the figures. As you go through the book, there will be lots of suggestions for increasing your income and reducing your spending, so this budget is something for you to come back to and refine.

In the meantime, if you have found you have a deficit each month, you need to start by trimming back your expenditure. Is there anything on your list you could live without or cut down on? Start by listing just the basic essentials for modern life: a roof over your head, just enough food in your cupboards, bills and transport. Then add other spending in order of priority until you reach your income level. This is now your monthly budget for the time being, until you find ways of increasing your income.

When you look at your list of expenses, is there anything that seems outrageous to you? How much are you spending on things like cappuccinos in the morning, chocolate at lunchtime, or a drink after work? And if you're a smoker, how much are you spending on your addiction? If you smoke 20 cigarettes a day, you're spending over a fiver a day on something that you are literally sending up in smoke! That's £35 a week, or £1,820 a year. Let me spell it out – over *one thousand eight hundred* pounds a year. Are you crazy? Your wallet and your lungs will be a lot healthier if you pack it in.

Is there some obvious overspend that if you could cut out, you could free up some cash for things that might make more sense in the long term? One of the benefits of writing your budget down is that it exposes the casual spending that can so easily get out of control. If you were to show your budget to someone else, is there something they'd be shocked by, or you'd be a bit ashamed of, or that you really can't justify? If the answer is yes, then take these things out and trim your budget.

Play around with your budget for a bit, see what you could live without or how much more you would need to earn before you break even. I want you to start to feel comfortable with the figures and the reality behind them. This is your budget and you need to feel a sense of ownership over it.

Peaks and troughs

Working out your monthly budget, or even your annual tally, isn't the only budgeting skill you need. Your earning and spending will not be the same throughout the year. You might have a big spike in your income with a Christmas bonus, or a big hike in your spending if your boiler packs up, so balancing your budget from month to month isn't enough.

Think for a moment about the kind of expenditure you encounter over a year that you might not have accounted for. A new bit of furniture, the children's school trips, holidays, getting the car through the MOT. It's inevitable that you will have months where you can't help but spend more than you earn, so the point of budgeting is to know where the extra money will come from. Are you putting enough by in the cheaper months to cover the expensive ones? If you're not, you're going to end up in debt.

In business, lots of companies keep quarterly accounts, which means they set their targets and budgets in three-month cycles. I think this is also a really good discipline for personal finances and I would recommend that you always try to end each quarter in profit.

The long-term view

Our peaks and troughs of income and expenditure continue throughout our lives so I'd encourage you to also keep another budget in mind – the long-term one. I'd like to use the example of a new business: often businesses are launched with loans that can see them thousands and thousands of pounds in the red; over the first few years, the business starts to make modest profits and the loan is slowly repaid, but then the business really finds its stride, profits increase and the loan is paid off.

Just like businesses, there are times when we need to borrow right up to our limit, and there are times when we start earning a better salary and have the chance to put something by. Being in debt is part of everyone's financial life and as long as you can afford the repayments to pay off your debts, you don't have to worry because you will be balancing your long-term budget.

You just have to make a distinction between your overall debt and your repayments on the loans. If you have a big loan or mortgage, your liabilities (your total debt) are likely to be less than your assets (your total wealth) – that's okay. What isn't okay is if you can't make the repayments on the loan that will eventually get you out of debt. Acquiring budgeting skills not only helps you work out what you can and cannot afford, it removes a lot of the fear and panic that so many of us associate with money.

 **CHECKLIST**

- ✔ Preparing a budget is the best way to know you're not overspending.
- ✔ Budgets aren't fixed – you can play around with them to help see how you can change your financial life.
- ✔ If you can't balance your budget month by month, you have to find a way of balancing your long-term budget.

4.
Some pounds are worth more than others

This might seem like an odd thing to say, but if you can get your head round the concept that some pounds are worth more than others, you can start making smarter decisions about what to do with your money – and your time. The thing to realise is that pounds don't just have a monetary value . . .

You've heard of the phrase 'time is money' and it's absolutely true. Let me give you an example of a freelance journalist who has the choice of taking on two pieces of work. Job A pays £500 and Job B pays £1,000. His first instinct is to take the piece of work that pays more, but Job B will take five days to complete, whereas he could do job A in a single day. As a daily rate, Job A actually pays two and a half times as much as Job B. So which one should he take?

If he has lots of offers of work, then it would probably make sense to do Job A because he will be available to take on other assignments for the rest of the week. However, if he's not getting much work, then he might as well earn the £1,000 because he wouldn't be doing anything productive with the rest of his week anyway. Your personal circumstance will always dictate how much of your time a pound is worth.

Although the 'time is money' phrase is well known, you don't ever hear people talking about the *emotional* value of money. Let me give you another example. Following the birth of his second child, an accountant wants to reduce his working hours to spend more time at home. He currently earns £50,000 a year working five days a week but has the opportunity to earn £35,000 a year at a different company working four days a week. Although his daily rate will be significantly lower taking the part-time job, it will give him the opportunity he craves not to miss out on seeing his young family grow up. Assuming he's budgeted for the drop in salary, then the lower-paid job is actually worth more to him than his current one. Simply chasing the highest-paying job isn't always the smartest choice and recognising the emotional value of money enables you to get what you want out of your financial choices.

Money also has *prestige* value. Let's go back to the freelance journalist for a moment. Imagine Job A still pays £500 and Job B pays £1,000 but they both take a week to complete. He'd be mad to take Job A, wouldn't he? Not necessarily. Let's say Job B is a pretty boring article in a magazine few people have heard of, but Job A is an exciting assignment for a national newspaper he hasn't written for before. The prestige of writing for a national newspaper, of getting his name in a reputable publication, and of impressing a new readership and a new editor with his talent may well be worth more than the extra £500 if he took Job B. Taking the lower-paid job might raise his profile, which in turn might impress influential people in his field and lead to more interesting work.

Money also has a *future* value. How often have you seen posters in the bank you've been with faithfully for years offering a really good introductory offer to new customers? Or how often have you been stuck in traffic behind a bus carrying a great big advert from your broadband company offering a phone/TV/broadband package that's a lot cheaper than the tariff you're paying – even when it's an ad for your broadband supplier! It happens a lot, doesn't it? But there are really good reasons why new customers often get the best deals. By tempting new customers with a discounted rate for a finite period, companies hope to keep their new clients when the discount period ends and they automatically switch to the standard rate. Discounting in the short term can make long-term sense.

So let's take an example of a plumber who has the choice of working privately for £30 an hour, or working for a property developer at £25 an hour. The developer can put a lot of business his way and by working cheaply for the developer, the plumber is pretty much guaranteeing himself lots of future work.

Finally, money also has a *convenience* value. Let's stick with plumbers. Let's say your boiler has broken down two days before Christmas and you call up several plumbers listed in Yellow Pages. One plumber says she can be with you in the New Year and that it will cost £30 to fix. Another plumber says he can be there within the hour but it will cost £80. I don't know about you, but that £80 quote sounds like a bargain in the circumstances.

The point of understanding that pounds don't just have a monetary value is to help you make smarter choices with money. As I've said before, being smart with money isn't just about a healthy bank balance, it's about getting what you want out of life and using the money you have to achieve your aims. If you can stop seeing money as a finite object and start seeing it in terms of what it can do for you, then you're on the right track.

CHECKLIST

✔ Learning to calculate the value of something, as opposed to its price, can help you prioritise your spending.

✔ Money doesn't just have a face value; it has an emotional value, a prestige value, a future value and a convenience value.

✔ Balancing these different criteria allows you to work out what something is really worth to you.

5.
What are *they* getting out of it?

Our financial lives are made up of a series of choices and negotiations. Whether we're buying a sofa or selling ourselves at a job interview, the decisions we make in almost every situation affect our financial well-being. How can we be sure if a deal we're being offered is too good to be true? How can we know what the real value of our purchases is? How can we work out if the electrician's quote is fair?

Being smart with money means always paying a fair price for whatever you buy and always charging a fair price for whatever you're selling. So how do you find out what a fair price is? After all, we can't be experts in banking and know if the mortgage we're being offered is the best we can get. We can't know everything about cars, pensions or any other field you care to mention. When you think about it, we're often in the position of being a layman negotiating with an expert: whatever transaction we're in, nine times out of ten the person we're dealing with will have more information and knowledge about the product, industry or situation than we do. So how can we possibly negotiate good deals and pay – or get – a fair price?

I have found that asking one simple question during every transaction I become involved with helps to level the playing field and allows me to work out the amount of money that should change hands: just ask yourself what *they're* getting out of it. If you enter transactions only thinking about what you're getting out of it, you're missing a trick. If you can put yourself in the other person's position, it lays the transaction bare and allows you to see more clearly exactly what's going on. And if you know what's going on, you can make smarter financial decisions.

Let's say you're talking to a financial adviser about taking out a pension. She's recommending a product from Company A even though it offers the same return as Company B. Now that might be because she's dealt with Company A a lot and knows that they're quick to process new accounts, or because they have a good track record. But if you ask her what she's getting out of it, you might uncover some interesting information. It might be that the commission Company A pays her for introducing new customers is higher than Company B would pay her. Can you still be sure that Company A's pension is the right product for you? If they're paying her such a nice commission, how can they afford to offer competitive rates? If you look at the small print, you might see there are higher management fees at Company A, or penalties for payment holidays that Company B doesn't charge. In the long term, you might be better off with Company B, but she's better off in the short term if she can persuade to put your money with Company A.

Now let's say that you're looking to buy a new car and the car you want has a list price of £10,000. You talk to the sales guy and he throws in a few extras to sweeten the deal and knocks £500 off the price. You might be tempted to sign there and then, but you shouldn't do anything until you've worked out what he's getting out of it. He's almost certainly on commission, so he'll get a little extra for selling you the car. Whether he sells it at £9,500 or £9,000 probably doesn't make a huge difference to his commission, and you can bet he'd rather have the commission on a £9,000 sale than no commission at all. So you have to try to work out what the lowest price he'll offer will be; if you can work out the point at which he still makes a profit, you've worked out how much you should be paying for the car.

So how do you do that? Well, you could try asking! You'd be surprised how often people will tell you. You might find out that if you buy the car using their finance option, he'll get another piece of commission, which might mean he'd be willing to knock a bit more off the price. Or perhaps if you pay straight away he can meet his quota and qualify for a bonus. What you need to establish is a negotiation that you both get something out of: he gets his commission and you get the car at the lowest possible price. Ask him how sales have been lately – if he tells you things are slow, you know you can probably bargain quite hard. So don't just walk round a showroom thinking about what extras you'd like thrown in, think about *why* the dealership will throw them in. If you ask as many questions about the salesman as you do about the car, you'll find out what he's getting out of it and uncover the true value of the car to him.

For me, the key to these kinds of negotiations is not to see the sales guy as a warrior you have to do combat with, but as a partner who you can work with. Let's see what happens when you get a quote from a gardener. Say he charges £20 an hour with a two-hour minimum once a fortnight. You've already had a few quotes so you know that £20 an hour is a reasonable amount to pay, so how can you get him to work for less? You could start by asking yourself what he would get out of working for you. In other words, what can you do for him? If he's just starting out, then you could offer to supply a reference that will help him get other work (and that way you can be sure he'll try to do a good job). Or maybe you can be flexible about the hours and days he works; flexibility can be very valuable to people running small businesses. Working out what is valuable to the person you are negotiating with helps you work out how much something is actually worth to you.

If you're selling something, this technique can work just as well. Imagine for a second you're the car salesman: what's the best way of finding the real budget a potential customer has? Ask questions. Are they in a hurry? Would they rather pay the list price and drive it away or wait for a lower price? Are they looking for something unique? If so, maybe they will pay extra for a bespoke respray. You just have to keep asking questions until you know exactly what the other person really wants out of a negotiation.

There truly isn't a situation where this technique doesn't produce results. Not only does it stop you wasting money and time, it helps you understand the person you're dealing with and lets you build a relationship with them. Good relationships where both parties benefit are so valuable to anyone in business that you can be sure you'll start your next negotiation with them from a much better position.

 **CHECKLIST**

✔ Finding out how other people benefit from your transaction is a sure way of making sure you get the maximum benefit.

✔ The best way to do this is through research, and the best method of research is asking questions.

✔ Good relationships are the foundation of good transactions.

6.
Get organised

One of the simplest ways to start getting more out of your money is to manage what you've got more effectively. Setting aside a little time to organise your finances in the short term will save you a lot of time in the long term.

I talk to a lot of new entrepreneurs who ask me for advice about starting a business. Over the years I have met thousands of people who tell me that they hate sitting down to do their accounts, they don't know how to keep accounts or they'd be happy to pay for someone else to look after their accounts for them. I have to tell them that unless they take their finances by the scruff of the neck, their businesses aren't likely to amount to much. The same is true for individuals: if money is a tool, you need to keep it oiled, cleaned and ready for action, and managing your money efficiently enables you to do that.

The basics

The first thing you have to do is keep track of your income and your outgoings. So instead of letting your wallet fill up with receipts, file them somewhere specific. Get a box or an in-tray where you can keep the advice slips from cash machines and credit card receipts.

Once a week, go through all the bits of paper and add up how much you've spent and see how it tallies with the budget you came up with in chapter 3. This shouldn't take you more than 15 minutes each week. You can do this on a spreadsheet or with pen and paper.

You'll be able to see if you've been overspending and if you'll need to cut back for the rest of the month, or if you're below budget, you'll know you can treat yourself. You should then keep the receipts until they've appeared on your bank statement or your credit card bill arrives – otherwise how can you be sure the bill is accurate? If the receipts are for anything valuable, hold on to them – they might help you get a refund in the future if an item is faulty, or it might help with an insurance claim.

The next thing to keep track of is direct debits and standing orders, and the easiest way to do this is with a current account that you manage online. If you don't have such an account, I really recommend you get one because you can check your statements whenever you like during the month. Take a look at your most recent bank statement and see who you pay money out to each month. The first thing to do is check that you are meant to be making all of those payments and that your old insurance company, or phone supplier, isn't still taking money out of your account each month. It's not unheard of, so do check that you are using the services you are being charged for.

I think it's a good idea to organise for all your direct debits and standing orders to leave your account on the same day. If you have a regular salary and the money from your employer always comes into your account at the end of the month, then arrange for your payments to all go out a couple of days later at the beginning of the next month. That way, you don't go through the month thinking you've got more money than you have.

Make a note of your pay day and always check your bank account to check the money has gone in. This is particularly important if you're self-employed and get paid erratically. When you agree to a piece of work, check when you will get paid for it and make a note in your diary to check the money has been transferred or the cheque has arrived. Keep a list of every contract you get, and tick them off when you receive payment – that way you won't forget about any unpaid invoices.

Banking

Once you've got yourself a current account that you can manage online, arrange for everything to be paid into that account. If you also use that account to pay for all your day-to-day needs, you will then have a record of all your income and expenditure in one place. Arranging an overdraft with your bank is a good idea, just in case of an unexpected payment or if you are late getting paid. However, overdrafts can cost money (see page 118), so make sure you arrange for one that you only pay for if you use it. My advice is to have an overdraft facility for half the amount of your monthly income. So if your net pay is £1,200 a month, don't ask for an overdraft of more than £600. That way any debt you incur will be in proportion to your income. And while you're talking to your bank, see what kind of interest they pay on your current account. You might find that you only get a higher rate if you're in credit, but you'll also pay a higher rate on your overdraft if you dip into the red. Ask your bank to calculate whether you'd be better off with a higher in-credit rate or a lower overdraft rate.

As well as your main current account, you may also need a few other types of accounts. If you are saving up for something, you should open a separate savings account. The different types of accounts are examined in the section on savings. If you are self-employed and will have tax and NI to pay on your earnings, it's really good discipline to open up another account to pay these contributions into when you get paid – that way you don't have to worry about how you will pay your tax bill. The same is true if you are VAT-registered – keep the money you'll owe the Inland Revenue in a separate account.

You might also find it helps to have one account for your personal spending and another for your household spending, especially if you share those expenses with someone else. Simply transfer in enough to cover your rent or mortgage, and bills, and then you know you're free to spend anything that's left in your personal account.

Records and reviews

However you manage your money, keeping records of your finances is important. Instead of throwing your bank statements in the bin, look at them, make sure they tally with your receipts and then file them. That way you can see how your spending pattern changes over the months, and over the years.

You should also review your finances regularly. Check that your savings are getting a good rate of interest, that you're not relying on your overdraft too much or that your direct debits are accurate. The great thing about internet banking and electronic transfers of money from your account to someone else's is that it's very easy, but when you never actually see the cash it's also easy to let it slip out of your grasp before you've even realised its gone. To be in control of your finances, you have to be engaged.

 **CHECKLIST**

- ✔ Get a current account that you can manage online.
- ✔ Keep a record of your spending.
- ✔ File your receipts and bank statements somewhere sensible.
- ✔ Always match your receipts to your bank and credit card statements.
- ✔ Review your finances regularly. It shouldn't take more than 15 minutes each week.

7.
It pays to stay informed

If **you want to succeed** in any walk of life, you need as much information to hand as possible. Information is ammunition, and the more of it you have, the smarter decisions you can make. With money, better information usually means bigger profits.

Getting your hands on financial information isn't hard and it doesn't cost you anything, yet so many people just don't engage with news from the financial world, probably because it's boring and they don't see what a difference it would make. Yet in the recent past, paying attention was hugely beneficial to thousands of people. In 2007, some smart people read that the property market was likely to be affected by the credit crunch and sold their properties and moved into rented accommodation while house prices fell. People who weren't paying attention ended up unable to sell their property in 2008 and just had to watch and wait as their homes lost value. In 2008, plenty of people read about the economic turmoil in Iceland and thought that taking their savings out of vulnerable Icelandic banks was a very good idea before Icesave, Kaupthing and Heritable Bank were declared insolvent. Even in less turbulent times, paying attention to the financial world will let you make the most of tax breaks, new products and undervalued investments. Believe me, it really does pay to stay informed.

It's important that you don't just rely on one source of information, whether it's your mate down the pub or a particular newspaper. To have reliable information, you need to gather it from as many sources as possible.

Watch the news

Just watching the evening news can give you an idea of what's happening in the financial world. Whether it's job losses or stock market rises, the big money news always makes the headlines. The problem is that very often we don't understand what we hear. Financial news is often reported with lots of jargon and isolated statistics so that it can be hard to work out the importance of a story and figure out how it affects us. When journalists talk about 'the underlying rate of inflation' or 'the FTSE dropped by 100 points today' it's easy to understand why so many people see the financial report as a cue to switch channels. (By the way, if there's any jargon you don't understand, turn to the Glossary at the back of this book.)

The thing is, I don't know why people expect to be able to understand it all. After all, if you went to night school to learn how to repair a car, you wouldn't expect to be able to know how to carry out a full service after your first lesson, would you? It takes time to absorb and understand complicated information, so the secret isn't just to watch the news once or twice, but to watch it every week – maybe even every night – so that over months (and maybe years), you start to understand more than you did and begin to spot patterns in financial behaviour.

The key to making sense of the money news is to ask yourself one very important question: how does that affect me? If you personalise the news it becomes more relevant and therefore easier to understand. For example, the next time the Bank of England changes interest rates, think about the impact it will have on you. Will your loan repayments change? Will your employer's costs go up or down? Will credit be easier to get, or harder? Will it boost or dampen the housing market? No matter what the headline is – a factory closing down, the pound dollar exchange rate, tax cuts – work out what it means for you, and then ask yourself if it means that you should be making changes. If you can't think of what a financial story means to you, think of who it does affect. Over time, you will become more financially aware and this will lead to becoming financially astute. And, of course, if there's still something you don't understand, there are plenty of other places you can look for information.

Newspapers

A s well as watching the television news, I think it pays to pick up a decent newspaper. As well as the stories that make it on to the TV news, newspapers report daily on issues relating to companies and the City. I'm amazed at how often I see people on the train flick over the business news and go straight to the TV listings or sports pages. I want to scream at them: 'Turn back a few pages – you might learn something that matters!'

At first, financial news in print can be just as confusing as anything you see on the TV, but the more you read, the more you will begin to understand. Often, newspapers will report on the reaction by business and banking leaders to the economic trends and events reported in the mainstream news; they will tell you the significance of these developments and explain how they will affect you.

Almost all the weekend editions of national and major regional newspapers have supplements on money. They usually follow up the week's big money stories and tend to have a consumer focus. So if the inflation rate has changed, you can be pretty sure that the weekend supplements will have articles on what you should do with your money in the light of the rate alteration.

Many also publish 'Best Buy' tables telling you which banks are offering the best savings, loans and mortgage rates so you can see easily how your financial products stack up against the market. If you do nothing else to improve your financial knowledge, read these weekend supplements. They're written for you, not for a City or banking readership, and they are full of truly relevant advice and simplified explanations of complex issues.

Other media

Even more information and advice is available in specialist money magazines, for example, *Money Week, Investors Chronicle, The Economist* etc. If you really want to swot up, take out a subscription to one of them. Some specialise in stock-market investments, others in business and companies – it may take a couple of issues to decide if any of them are right for you. If you are thinking of buying shares, especially if you intend to do so without the help of a broker (see the Savings and Investment section), then a few quid spent on a specialist magazine could be the best money you ever part company with, after this book of course.

Financial journals might not be the only specialist maga-zines of use to you. If you work in a particular sector, reading the relevant trade publication will really boost your knowledge of the big players and issues in your industry. This information can help you land a better job, identify trends and boost your earning power.

Satellite TV is full of 24-hour news channels, all of which carry financial news. Most have a weekly magazine show focusing on economic issues while some – like Bloomberg and CNBC – are dedicated to covering the ups and downs of the financial news. And don't forget radio, where phone-in shows can give you specific advice on your financial concerns.

Internet

The biggest and most accessible financial resource is, of course, the internet. Whether you want to look up a defini-tion of 'index-linked inflation' or see how the Dow Jones index is performing, it's all just a few clicks away.

The problem with the internet is that it can also be as un-reliable as it is helpful! There's a lot of inaccurate and biased information out there, so it makes sense to stick to reliable sources of information – the BBC, a trusted newspaper, or an established online magazine like Motley Fool (www.fool.co.uk). Don't just rely on one source; always get a second opinion on financial news and trends from other sites and services.

Financial advisers

My other tip – and possibly my best tip – for keeping informed is to go and see a financial adviser regularly. It's usually possible to have an initial meeting with an IFA (Independent Financial Adviser) for free and it's a great opportunity to ask questions. 'So, what do you think of pensions in the current climate?' 'Are there any tax advantages I could benefit from?' 'Who's offering the best ISAs this year?'

Obviously, you're not always going to get a straightforward reply ('I'd need to look carefully at your financial position before I could recommend an ISA product . . .'), but you'll probably hear something that will guide your thoughts. Perhaps you'll learn that the ISA market is getting very com-petitive or if you wait till the end of the tax year, you might get a better deal. You don't have to become their client to be steered in the right direction.

You can find your nearest IFA at www.unbiased.co.uk, and I think that if you go and see a handful of IFAs on the pretext of wanting investment/pension/tax advice, you will start to build up a store of the kind of information known only to financial professionals. No matter how much research you do into the world of finance, you're unlikely to do it full time, which of course is what IFAs do. If you're lucky, you might come across an adviser who seems genuinely knowledgeable and on the ball and you might ask them to look after your financial decisions. However, by the end of this book, you should feel confident to make your money choices without outside help.

CHECKLIST

- ✔ The more information you have, the better decisions you can make.
- ✔ Don't rely on one source for your information.
- ✔ Set up preliminary meetings with IFAs and ask a lot of questions.

8.
Know the cycles

There's one last concept to digest before we move on to the practical issues surrounding the five key financial mechanisms of earning, spending, borrowing, saving and investing and that's understanding that money is affected by two very powerful cycles.

The economic cycle

You will have heard people talk about 'boom and bust' when it comes to the economy, and no matter what any politician tells you, no matter what financial legislation is passed, the economy will always have peaks and troughs. Knowing where the economy is headed is the absolute key to making smarter decisions about money, and ultimately making more of it.

The reasons why I think we'll never be free of the cycle of boom and bust is because it's embedded in human nature. When Peter sees Paul making money fishing in the lake, he's going to fish in the lake too. Gradually we all start fishing in the lake and we all make money, the price of land around the lake soars and the restaurant owners near the docks do well. Eventually, there are fewer and fewer fish left in the lake, profits drop, people sell their boats and move on to the next boom, the restaurants go out of business and the fish will be left in peace to breed. And when the numbers of fish reach a certain level again, Peter's and Paul's grandchildren will be buying boats and go through exactly the same cycle all over again.

If governments try to stop this boom and bust through legislation, people will just go and find a different lake. It's very hard to stand by and watch another person, a rival company or a foreign country, profit from a situation and not want to be allowed to profit from it yourself. Any government that tries to be restrictive knows its brightest and best people – the same people who really add value to any economy – will take their talent to somewhere where they're allowed to make money.

So to be overly simplistic about this, the key to knowing which way the economy is going is to know how many fish are left in the lake. Is the sector you work in on the up or about to hit a brick wall? How much growth is left in your industry? If demand is growing, if prices are rising, your business is booming. If demand is wavering, if people can't afford what you're selling, you're on the brink of a bust.

Odd as it sounds, recessions bring opportunities to be smart with money, whether it's buying property when prices are low, picking up bankrupt stock at auction, snapping up undervalued shares or just buying a car for well below the list price. Recessions generally weed out the weak companies with poor management, which in turn gives better-run organisations a chance to acquire their rivals' customers easily and cheaply. Equally, a strong pound gives importers a chance to maximise profits, while a weak pound is a boon for exporters and the domestic tourist industry. As they say, where there's pain, there's also gain (if you know where to look for it).

Knowing where you are in the economic cycle can help you assess the risks you are taking with your financial decisions. If things are on the way up, your exposure to risk is minimal because it's easier to make money in a boom. If things are looking dicey, then you're taking a risk if you commit cash or time to a new venture or investment. If you understand the cycles, then you can make smarter decisions about *when* to do something with your money as well as what to do with it.

Your personal cycle

No matter what happens with the wider economy, there are times in every human lifespan when it makes more sense to speculate, and times when it's advantageous to accumulate. Working out *what* you want and *when* you'll want it is the foundation of smarter choices.

Broadly, the younger you are, the more scope you have for taking risks. The fewer responsibilities you have, the freer you are to give something a go. The older you get, the more commitments you have, and you have less time for the effects of compound returns to have an effect on your investments. Consequently the more responsible you have to be with your money.

Your age will affect your long-term financial planning. Any IFA will tell you that the younger you are, the smaller the monthly contributions you'll need to make to end up with a decent pension. That's because the £50 a month you save at 20 accrues 10 years' worth of compound interest that the £50 you put away at 30 doesn't earn. Equally, buying a property when you're young – even if it seems like a stretch – means you benefit from house price growth for longer. You might be worried about house prices falling, but with youth on your side, you should be able to ride out any short-term downturn. See the chapters on Property for more detailed advice on this.

Our earnings also go in cycles. If you take your working life as being from 20 to 60 years of age, you'd probably expect to earn more in your thirties than you did in your twenties because you'll have had a few promotions and pay rises. For many people, their forties is when they really earn good money as they achieve senior management level, and often this is followed by a drop in earnings in their fifties when their skills are overtaken by the next generation.

Thankfully this rough pattern generally mirrors our increased demand for money: in our thirties and forties we tend to start families and incur all the expenses that this entails:

a bigger house, bigger car, bigger food bills. In our fifties, however, our mortgages tend to be smaller or non-existent because we downsize to a smaller house when the kids have left home.

The point is, there are times in our life when we are in a position to make the most of the opportunities the wider economy offers us, and there are times when it's smarter to be more cautious. Understanding these cycles stops us from making mistakes and enables us to capitalise on opportunity.

CHECKLIST

- ✔ Understanding the effects of the economic cycle and your personal cycle on money enables you to seize on the right opportunities.

- ✔ Even downturns in the economy create opportunities to make and save money.

- ✔ Being smart with money isn't just about what you do with it, it's also about when you do it.

PART TWO
Getting more money

1.
Maximise your salary

et me start with a blindingly obvious fact: the more money you can get your hands on, the more chances you give yourself to do something really smart with it. This part of the book is all about accruing as much money as you can, but before I go any further, I really want to say something about your work/life balance. I don't want you to think that the only important thing about a job is how much it pays. A fulfilling career where you do work you're proud of, enjoy the company of your co-workers and have enough time left for the other things in life that matter are all key factors that should be balanced with your salary package. I'm going to talk a lot about maximising your earnings, but please don't think this means I believe that earning megabucks is more important that being happy with your career. Although I think there are a handful circumstances in which it can be smart to just take the money even if you don't like the work very much – we'll come to those at the end of this section – I want to make it clear that the advice over the next few pages should be considered in the light of how much fulfilment your work offers and how it fits in with the rest of your life.

That said, a salaried job is how most Britons acquire money so it's absolutely crucial to your financial well-being to make sure you are a) earning enough to live on; b) being paid fairly for your efforts.

Do you earn enough?

Spending years of your career in a job that pays below the market rate, or spending several years wasting your earning power in casual jobs has a massive impact on your long-term financial health. You need to be sure that the work that you do supports your lifestyle, and ideally, lays the foundations to be able to earn well in the future.

So let's start with a simple question: how much do you earn? It sounds like a straightforward question but it's not always that easy to answer it. Have you noticed that most job adverts offer £X an hour or an annual salary of £XX,000? I don't know about you, but I don't have many hourly or annual expenses, so telling me how much you will pay me each year isn't particularly helpful – how do I know if it's enough to pay for everything I need?

Given that most of our expenses are monthly – certainly the big ones like mortgage and rent payments, council tax and loan repayments – working out your monthly income is probably the most useful way of working out if you earn enough. So if you're thinking of taking a job that pays £20 an hour for 40 hours a week, you will earn approximately £3,440 a month. Or will you?

You need to calculate your tax and NICs and deduct them from your total. The TUC has a really useful website with a tax calculator you can use at www.worksmart.org.uk/tools/tax_calc.php, so if you want to skip the next few paragraphs (there's a bit of maths coming up), please make sure you take a look at the tax calculator because it's a very useful tool. In the meantime, this is my rough guide to working out how much money will actually be paid to you.

Start by working out your annual salary by multiplying your monthly income by 12, which in the case above gives you a salary of £41,280 a year. The next thing to do is deduct your tax-free allowance from that annual total. This amount varies according to your tax code, which you can find on your payslips and P60 forms, but the standard amount is £6,035 a year.

As you don't pay tax on approximately the first £6,000, your taxable income is reduced to £35,245. According the 2008/09 figures, you pay 20% tax on the first £34,800 of your taxable income, which works out at £6,960. (You pay 40% tax on any earnings over £40,835, i.e. the tax-free amount of £6,035 plus £34,800, which in this case means 40% of £445, or £178. So your total tax is £6,960 plus £178, or £7,138.)

NICs also take a bit of working out and differ between employed and self-employed workers and whether your NICs go straight into a pension. Most employees pay 11% of their earnings between £105 and £770 a week, and 1% on everything above that. According to the worksmart.org.uk tax calculator, an employed person would pay £3,816 in NICs on a salary of £41,280. That means the total deductions from your annual income of £41,280 are £7,138 in tax and £3,816 in NICs which leaves you with £30,326. To get your net monthly income, you just have to divide by 12. So now you know that £20 an hour means a monthly income of £2,527. As you've already worked out your monthly budget in the Budgeting chapter, you can make a decision as to whether or not this salary is enough for you to live on.

Gross income	£41,280
Taxable income (less allowance)	£35,245
20% tax on first £34,800	£6,960
40% tax on earnings over £40,835	£178
NICs	£3,816
Net income	£30,326

If that was a little too much like a maths class, I apologise. The point I want to get across is that you can only know if you're earning enough if you know what you're actually getting in your pocket each month. It should be clear to see how easy it is to stumble along thinking that you're earning enough money, only to find out later that you've slowly been going further and further into the red. So before you read any further, take a moment to check your sums.

Do you earn enough?

It's the same question, but this time I'm looking for a completely different kind of answer. How can you be sure that the salary you are paid is good enough? How can you be sure you're not being underpaid? This is a really serious question because if you spend several years in a job in which you're not earning to your full potential, it can really compromise your financial future.

If you aren't earning at the right level, the impact will be felt throughout your life. If you think that's a bit strong, think about it for a second. If you are underpaid, it will affect things like how big a mortgage you can take out, which affects the sort of home you can buy, which may make property a worse long-term investment for you. If your employer contributes a percentage of your salary to a pension scheme, they are putting in less than they should. Earning below your potential affects how much you can save, and of course what you can buy with your hard-earned cash. Making sure you're being paid enough is really important.

The first thing to do to check the going rate in your industry is to put 'salary checker' into Google. You'll get loads of possibilities and you should try out several. Key in your occupation, age and other details and the salary checker will instantly tell you what it thinks you should be earning. Of course, it's just a guide. A little program on a website can't compute the value of your qualifications, your specialist knowledge, your company's health insurance package or know exactly what your job entails, but it's a quick way of getting a rough ballpark figure. Many of the big recruitment agencies carry out surveys into salaries, so while you're online, also search for 'salary survey' and see what the latest figures for your industry are.

The next place to check is your HR department. Many companies structure the salaries they offer within pay grades; this information isn't usually secret even if individual salaries are. It's possible that the salaries they are offering new staff are higher than those they pay existing members of the team, so check that you are being paid what you should be. A word of warning though: check whether figures include bonuses and benefits, and make sure you're comparing like with like. You should also look at recruitment ads and see what salaries are being offered for similar jobs elsewhere.

Finally, ask your co-workers. I know it's not something we usually talk about in Britain but if it's appropriate, this is the best way of making sure that you are not being paid less than the person sitting at the next desk.

If your investigations have led you to believe that you are being underpaid, you have three courses of action. Firstly, you could just live with it, but for the reasons outlined above, this won't help your long-term financial position. Secondly, you could ask for and negotiate a pay rise; and thirdly you could look around for a better-paid job.

To successfully persuade your employer that you are worth more than they are currently paying you, you need to offer them some proof. It is reasonable to expect to be paid more for taking on more responsibility or for working longer hours, so if either of those situations is relevant to you, you might be able to make a case for a pay rise. Simply telling your boss that he or she isn't paying the going rate is likely to get his or her back up and get your negotiations off to a bad start. If my staff started saying things like that, I would tell them that *I* decide the salary levels and if they're not happy with their income, they should feel free to look for other work!

A good reason to ask for more money is if you've never had a pay rise since you started working for the company. Most employers recognise that earnings need to rise roughly in line with inflation when profits allow, and if your pay hasn't been increased for several years, this might just be an oversight. Ask for a performance and pay review – and be prepared to be told that pay rises are only awarded on merit. In my view, you should be willing to work harder to get paid more.

Timing your request for a pay rise may play a big part in whether or not you would get one. If your company has just lost a major contract – whether or not it's got anything to do with your individual performance – or when your bosses are making staff redundant, you're not likely to get a positive response. Indeed, in economic downturns, many workers have historically accepted a pay cut so that they can keep their jobs while their employer struggles. However, if your company is booming, if new contracts are being signed every week, then you're far more likely to have your request viewed favourably.

If a pay rise isn't an option, you could look for a better-paid job with another company. If you are successful in approaching other employers and are asked in for an interview, my advice is never to tell them that the reason you want to work for them is because they pay well! Always talk about the challenges of a new position, the opportunities you think they offer and how you would relish working for such a good organisation! Trust me, it might be smart to move jobs to get the salary you deserve, but it doesn't impress a potential employer if you tell them that's why you want to join their workforce.

Do you earn enough?

No, you haven't misread it – it is the same question again, and again it needs a different answer. So far we've talked about making sure you earn enough in your current job or career, but what about if you are in completely the wrong career?

Given that it's likely that the majority of the money you receive in your life will be from employment, it might be smart to think about whether or not you're in the right kind of employment. There are no hard and fast rules about what is the most lucrative career choice – in some industries, the entry-level salaries are tiny but as you climb the ladder your income can soar – but regularly analysing your career progress is a good habit to get into. I know so many people who didn't pay attention to their careers – they were happy just to take the pay cheque and enjoy the work – and found out too late that their best earning years were behind them.

At least once a year, I think you should sit down and answer the following questions:

- Should I be asking for a pay rise?
- What opportunities does my current employer offer me for advancement?
- What is my likely next career move?
- What kind of salaries are on offer at the next level up?
- Should I improve my skill set with some training?
- What are the barriers to advancement and how can I over-come them?

If you ask yourself these questions, the answers will prevent your career from stagnating and your earnings falling below what you ought to be paid. This isn't a careers advice book, but if your answers to these questions make you question your immediate professional future, then maybe you should buy one.

Of course there are some careers that are never going to pay as well as others. Nursing and teaching, for example, offer a good deal of job security but nothing like the salaries available in areas like banking and technology. If the profession you're in doesn't offer the earning potential you're after, you need to think about whether or not you would be better off if you changed careers. It's not easy to go from one industry to another and career changers often find themselves competing with younger (and cheaper) applicants for jobs in their new profession, but a short-term drop in earnings might deliver long-term rewards. Or you might want to think about starting your own business.

Always be thinking about where your career is heading and not just about the current position you have. If you fail to pay attention to your career, you are missing out on income that should be yours for the taking. If you look around inside your company and don't see anyone earning a decent wage, if you see that someone like you wouldn't be considered for promotion, then I strongly urge you to take your career – and your earning power – in hand and make some changes before it's too late.

CHECKLIST

✔ Maximising your income from your salary can have a big impact on your long-term wealth.

✔ Check that you are being paid the going rate.

✔ Ask yourself if it's time to ask for a pay rise and/or a promotion.

✔ Consider if your profession offers good enough financial prospects.

✔ Don't let your career drift – keep thinking about your next career move.

2.
Boost your income

As well as looking to your career as a route to further income, it might pay to focus on some other ways you can boost the amount you have coming in each month. Some of the suggestions here won't lead to untold riches, but as they involve hardly any effort on your part, I think they're really worth looking into. Added together, these options could lead to a genuine rise in your income. One in particular, could transform your financial future .

Tax credits and benefits

If you are single and in full-time employment and earn under £12,800 a year, there might be help available from the government in the form of tax credits. If you have children, there might be even more money available: if your household income is below £58,000 a year and you pay for childcare, you should definitely look at www.direct.gov.uk and investigate your entitlement.

The tax credit system is complicated, but for those in regular employment it can offer rebates on the amount of tax you pay each month, meaning more money is in your pocket than the Treasury's coffers. Don't let the fact that it's complicated put you off. You can find out quickly online if you're entitled to the credits and it could be worth hundreds of pounds to you each month.

You might also be entitled to receive some benefits that you're not claiming. It's estimated that billions of pounds of benefits aren't claimed each year, presumably because people didn't realise they were entitled to claim. If you are on a low income, you could get help with paying your rent and council tax, and if you have kids, child benefit could boost your household's coffers. Find out what's available at your local Citizens Advice Bureau or JobCentrePlus.

Tax credits and benefits won't change your life or make you rich, but that's no reason not to claim them. It's like walking down the street and walking past a man who's handing out £5 notes and not taking one if you don't claim what's yours. If you claim it, you can choose what you want to do with it, and it might make enough of a difference to let you save some, so that these incremental increases in your income accrue to become a meaningful amount.

Employee benefits

There may be another source of additional income you'd be mad to miss out on: check if your employer provides staff with additional benefits. Some companies offer things like health insurance and life cover, so there would be no point in you paying for these things privately. Some also make pension contributions, which may mean you can reduce the amount you contribute. You might find there are things like interest-free loans to pay for your annual travel (thereby saving you a tidy sum on paying for a monthly travel pass), or they might have negotiated special deals with local shops, restaurants and businesses. Recently, the government brought in legislation to encourage more people to cycle to work, and if your employer signed up to the scheme, you might be able to buy a bicycle for half price. There might be share option schemes you could join, but the big winner for employees is their annual bonus. Make sure you know what you would have to do to qualify for a bonus – and then make sure you do the necessary to ensure it becomes payable. The other thing to check is whether or not your employer has an overtime policy as it's just possible that those extra hours you've put in mean that you're due an extra payment. Missing out on these sources of income is something no smart employee should do.

eBay

You can sell almost anything on eBay and I reckon most people in Britain could use it to produce a bit of extra cash. Whether it's a book you're never going to read again, a DVD you've finished with or tools gathering dust in the shed, www.eBay.co.uk is the world's shop where buyers and sellers trade everything under the sun.

I was recently renovating a hotel and my builder gave me a quote for £2,000 to dismantle and take an old greenhouse away. I told him to stick it on eBay and a few weeks later, not only did someone come round and dismantle the greenhouse, but they gave me £300 for it! We also had a piano at the hotel that we didn't want: my builder gave me a quote of £30 to take it away, so I stuck it on eBay and sold it for £200.

Whether you sell at eBay or car-boot sales, I bet your home is full of stuff you could live without.

VAT

This option isn't open to everyone, but if you are freelance or run a small company, you may benefit from registering for VAT (Value Added Tax), a tax which can be charged on all the goods and services you sell. The rate of VAT depends on your industry and current government policy, but the rate for most goods and services is usually 17.5% (although this was reduced from December 2008 for 13 months to 15% in an attempt to boost the economy).

If your turnover is above £67,000 (2008/09 figures), you are obliged to register for VAT, but you can make a voluntary registration if your income is below that. Although it's a bit complicated and requires a little bit of paperwork, you might find you are significantly better off because registering for VAT allows you to claim back the VAT you pay out on your purchases. So if you have expenses of £1,000 on which you've been charged 17.5% – or £175 – you can claim that amount back from the Inland Revenue against the VAT you charge on your goods and services. Most freelance people I know benefit from registering, because even if they don't have many expenses to claim the VAT back on, they still charge VAT on their services, meaning they get to bank an extra 17.5%, which sits in their bank account earning interest until they have to pay the balance to the Inland Revenue.

What many people don't realise is that they could be even better off if they registered to pay VAT on a flat rate, which is usually advantageous if you don't incur many expenses. The sector you work in will determine the flat rate you will be asked to pay. In a few sectors, the rate is as low as 2%, and there are quite a few sectors where it's 5% or 6%. Check www.hmrc.gov.uk to see whether you fit the criteria for the flat rate scheme (for example, your turnover must be below £150,000).

The VAT you owe is calculated slightly differently if you're on the flat rate. Let me give you an example, assuming the rate for your industry is 9.5%:

You do a piece of work for £1,000 and invoice your clients for £1,175 (i.e. £1,000 + VAT). When you do your VAT return, you will be asked to hand over 9.5% of the total turnover instead of deducting the VAT you've paid on purchases from the VAT you've been paid on your sales. In this case, it works out at £111.62. In this example – which assumes you don't have any expenses – you'd have boosted your income by over £63, which is 6.3% on top of the £1,000 you originally charged. That's a better return than you'd get in a bank and more than most employers would offer as a pay rise. And if your industry's rate was 6%, you would be £104.50 better off – it's like giving yourself a 10.45% pay rise!

If you make a lot of purchases, registering for the flat rate might not be sensible, but I think this is certainly worth talking over with the VAT office or an accountant.

Get a second job

If the suggestions so far have involved minimal effort on your part for modest returns, this one may involve a superhuman effort – but it might bring in the level of income that could transform your financial health.

If you feel that you can't earn any more at work, then you could consider taking on a second job. If you worked the evening shift in your local pub, for example, you might earn a couple of hundred extra a week – and you could still hang out with your mates. Plus, you wouldn't have any time to spend the money so you could really power up your savings. If you work shifts and can't commit to regular hours, why not consider something like driving a cab? I drove cabs for a large part of my twenties and it was a huge boost to the money I was earning as a mechanic.

It seems that every other time I get stopped at traffic lights, there's a sign tied to a lamppost saying, 'Earn £££ in your spare time working from home'. Although these schemes are usually bogus, there certainly are ways you can earn a bit extra in your spare time – whether it's trading on eBay, driving a cab or taking in a lodger (you can earn up to £4,250 tax-free under the government's Rent a Room scheme).

I think there are times in our life when we owe it to ourselves to work as hard as we can. If you are young and fit and don't yet have the commitment of children, I can't think of many reasons why you wouldn't want to stockpile as much cash as you can to prepare for your future. If you're saving up for something specific, why not use that desire to spur you on to put in some extra hours and get some cash flowing into your bank account.

It's not sustainable to work long hours for ever, but if you are at a time in your life when you are watching TV when you could be working, you are missing out on a significant source of income. If you pass up the opportunity to earn the cash while you can, that's money you're letting slip through your fingers just as surely as if you were dropping it on the pavement.

CHECKLIST

✔ There are several ways you can boost your income for very little effort.

✔ Everyone can free up some cash by selling on eBay.

✔ Getting a second job can bring home a significant additional income.

3.
Lifetime earnings

So far I've focused a lot on monthly earnings and balancing budgets in the short term. In this chapter I want to get you thinking about your lifetime earnings and to see your current income as part of a bigger financial picture. As your career is likely to be the major source of income you have in your life, it's vital you maximise your earning power by understanding the patterns of earning that exist in your industry. It's important for another reason too, because when your income fluctuates over time, you don't just have to think about balancing your budget each month, or even each year, you need to start building a picture of your lifetime budget.

For a few decades after World War II, a fairly standard pattern of work emerged, particularly for men. After school, you got a junior job in a good company, slowly climbed the management ladder and enjoyed a pay rise with each promotion before retiring with a company pension that provided a decent standard of living.

If there was a graph of lifetime earnings it would have looked something like the one at the top of the next page.

There was a certainty that, even if you didn't earn more, you would never earn less, and the unions meant entire generations felt the security of a job for life. Times have changed and our workforce is now more responsive to economic fluctuations and is more mobile. These days, to get a toehold in some of the more lucrative professions you're supposed to serve a poorly paid apprenticeship for a couple of years before leaping up the income scale until redundancy intervenes in your mid-forties and you struggle from then until retirement to earn at the level

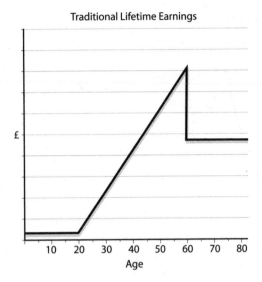

Traditional Lifetime Earnings

you've become accustomed to. These days, many workers' income graphs look more like the one opposite.

Government statistics in the Annual Survey of Hours and Earnings (2008) showed that the best earning decade for men was between the ages of 40 and 49, while for women it was between 30 and 39. Different industries have different earning curves and the key to earning the most money you can in your career is to identify the likely earning curve in your sector so that you can be in a position to benefit. For the next couple of pages, I want you to think about the earning opportunities your industry offers.

Perhaps the best example of someone with a pronounced earnings curve (as opposed to a straight line) is a young Premiership footballer. He might be a millionaire by the time he's 20 but never work again after getting injured at 24. In the space of a few years, he'll earn all the money he'll ever earn and will have to live off savings and investments for the rest of his life. And when I see those celebrity magazines with a soap actor or a pop star's wedding, I completely understand why someone whose career is likely to be short capitalises on their

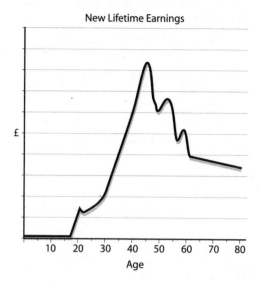

New Lifetime Earnings

fame by selling their wedding photos while they're a saleable commodity.

While these are extreme examples, there are now many people who, although they earn well, earn their money in fits and starts. I've met TV producers, property developers and plumbers who earn their money on a deal-by-deal basis. Within that curve of earnings on the second graph, their income spikes up and down like a heartbeat on a hospital monitor. They don't have to budget like footballers who earn all their money in the space of a few years, but they have to budget for the lean year that follows the boom one, or the year of preparation before they can start work on their next project. For every smart budgeter I know who calculates how much they need to put aside, I know another one who blows their money as soon as they earn it and are virtually penniless between paydays.

With more and more of us earning our money in fits and starts and peaks and troughs, we need to acquire new skills to ensure our financial well-being in the long term. While none of us know what we'll be earning in the future, we can try our best to anticipate our likely earning curve. We do that by looking at the career structures in the industry we're in and seeing how likely it is that our path will follow the standard pattern.

Let's take another look at the second graph. This could be your earning pattern if you take a look around your office and don't see too many grey heads. You wouldn't be a fool if you anticipated that at a certain age you'll also be likely to 'disappear' from your industry. Even though it might have taken till your early thirties to start earning decent money, you can anticipate that your window for earning a big salary is relatively short, perhaps only fifteen years or so. Knowing this, it would be smart to plan for a drop in earnings in your forties. What might that mean in practice? Perhaps planning to have paid your mortgage off by the age of 45, or not taking on debts in your forties that you won't be able to repay, or working out how you might use your skills in a future outside your current career structure. What this graph might also tell you is that there is a time to take on a bigger mortgage when you will be able to cope with the repayments.

Or this graph might reassure people in their twenties that a decent income lies ahead and although they don't have enough right now to save or invest, they're likely to see an income surge in the next few years that will open up their financial choices. I urge you to look at the people you know in your profession and plot out your own likely earnings graph, because timing a financial decision correctly is a big part of it being a smart financial decision.

Promotions and career ladders

Such an earnings curve might also tell you that if you get to your late twenties and haven't got yourself in the sort of position where you can start landing the jobs that will define your career, then it might be time to start taking your job seriously – if you miss the big salary boat it will have a huge impact on not just your lifetime earnings, but your life-long wealth. Although it's unfair and unreasonable, most employers look to employ the same sorts of people in the same sorts of jobs. It differs from industry to industry, but roughly speaking in your late twenties and early thirties you move up the ladder, taking on bigger jobs with bigger salaries. If you miss out on this period of promotion, there's a real chance you will always miss out on the promotions that are appropriate for your age.

A good illustration of this is when people retrain in their thirties and forties in a new field and become as well-qualified as a 20-year-old in their new field. Employers are likely to favour the 20-year-old because their youth means they might get a longer service out of them (and they'll probably work for less), yet the retrainers are too old for the middle-management positions that are often held by people in their late twenties and early thirties. They don't fit into the expectations of their new profession and find it hard to get work. It's a similar story for a lot of women who spend key years of their career raising a family. They often miss out on the promotions their male colleagues are in line for in their late twenties and early thirties, so that when the promotions to more senior management are made a little later in their lives, it's the men who are in a posi-tion to be considered (which explains why women's earnings peak in their thirties and men's in their forties). As rotten as it sounds, this is unfortunately the way a lot of industries work, so one of the smartest things you can do in relation to money is to position yourself to earn as much of it as possible at the right time in your life, which means taking your career seriously. If you don't, your earning curve might look like the graph on the following page.

We've probably all worked in organisations where there's a handful of older people still working on the shopfloor who have seen younger people get promoted ahead of them. They missed out on their moment for promotion and they are now considered 'too old' for it because they don't fit their com-pany's image of who should get promoted! It's unfair, but it's

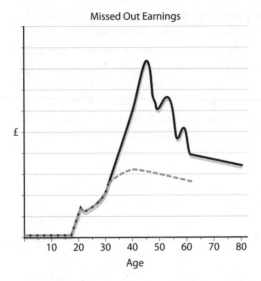

also reality. Companies aren't often very flexible and they have corporate cultures that can be hard to change, which is why managers often promote in their own image. The key thing I'm saying here is to identify your important career moments and make sure you don't miss them.

Parental leave

When your children are little, one of the major costs is childcare. Although you can get government help for this, it can still be incredibly expensive. I was talking to a friend recently who earns £60,000 a year, which meant she didn't qualify for government help. As a high-earning professional, she felt that familiar conflict between wanting to look after her daughter and setting an example that women can be bread-winners, but in the end she decided to return to work and hired a nanny. The going rate for nannies in her area was a staggering £30,000 a year, plus the employer's NICs she had to pay on top of this, not to mention increased insurance premiums because her home was now a place of work. She reckoned it cost her about £35,000 to pay someone to look after her child, but after tax and NI were deducted from her pay packet, her net salary was worth about £42,000. She was effectively going back to work for a take-home pay of £7,000 a year.

I'm including this story because she told me that she was seriously thinking of giving up work. I told her that, financially, it would be the wrong thing to do because taking three or four years out of her career at a time when her contemporaries were bagging promotions would put a dent in her lifetime earnings. In other words, the pain of returning to work for such a small gain would be rewarded with higher lifetime earnings that would make the cost of childcare seem very affordable when set against the cost of lost income.

What if you missed your moment?

I realise that the previous couple of pages may have made depressing reading for anyone who wonders why they've never moved up the earnings scale. Logically, most people will miss out on their promotion moment because in every organisation there are always fewer managers than there are staff. If you now recognise that you're being passed over for promotion because you don't fit your company's, or your industry's, profile for promotion, the first thing you should do is stop waiting for promotion. The chances are it won't happen, so hanging around waiting for a promotion on the basis of long service means working for years earning below your potential. We can't all move up the ladder, so what else can you do to increase your salary potential?

One thing to consider is to specialise. Companies need specialists as well as managers. Ask yourself if there's an area of your work that you enjoy and would be happy to work harder at, or study further, to become an expert in. Can you identify trends in your industry that will make one particular skill or one piece of technology essential for future success? If you have several years' experience in a sector, you're likely to know something about what is valuable to that sector. Specialists are very valuable to companies and industries, and are consequently paid relatively well.

However, perhaps you need to look outside your career to boost your wealth. Whether it's savings, investments, property or starting a business, if you can see that your job earnings may remain stunted at a certain level, you should start looking at the other financial options that are covered later in this book.

Economic curves

The other element of lifetime earnings is the wider economy. As I've already said, I think booms and busts are part of human nature, so no matter which political party comes into power, the economy will always run in cycles. So just as there are times in your career when your earnings can really motor, there are times in the economic cycle when it makes sense to earn money while you can. If your big earning years coincide with a boom in the economy, you have a real opportunity to earn financial security for yourself. Every economic cycle presents us with opportunities, and if you start looking for them, they're not hard to find.

There are moments in our careers when we have to seize opportunities and there are times when you just have to take a chance. Every generation gets a chance, and the smart people make sure they don't miss out. Take the computer boom in the US in the 1960s and 70s. The guys who founded companies like Hewlett Packard, Apple Macintosh and Microsoft were all born within a few years of each other. It was their moment and they took it. More recently, if you look at the dotcom boom in the late 1990s, it seemed every entrepreneur who was profiled in the press was aged between 27 and 29. There was a reason for this: at that age they had acquired enough knowledge and skills to start a business, but not yet had the promotions and salaries that they couldn't risk giving up or the responsibilities of families to make them think twice. Of course, it's not just those entrepreneurs who benefited – the people who went to work for them and the companies that supplied them with everything from coffee cups to accountancy services did well too. You don't have to be an entrepreneur to benefit from the swings and roundabouts in the economic cycle, you just have to pay attention and jump on board at the right moment. Sometimes these economic opportunities are created by technology, sometimes by legislation, sometimes by demographics. The more you read about your industry and the economy, the more you engage with the information that's all around us, and the more likely it will be that you spot and seize your moment.

The point of getting you to think about your lifetime earnings is so you realise that there are times when it's smarter to take risks and times when the smart people are more cautious. When we come on to talk about spending, saving and investing, you'll realise that knowing where you are on your personal earnings graph is a vital part of making smarter decisions with your money.

In every career there are opportunities, maybe for promotion or to specialise in new technology, or perhaps when your reputation means that the work comes to you and you can charge what you want for your skills. Recognising these moments and building on the momentum that accompanies them can transform your earnings. I would reiterate that if you're young and don't have the responsibility of providing for a family, then this would be the time to work long hours and stockpile the cash. If you find that you've caught the promotion wave and your earnings are booming, I would suggest that you would do well to stifle your desire for a career change for a few years. And if you're a footballer or a WAG, you should sell your wedding photos while the money is on offer!

CHECKLIST

- ✔ Very few people have a job for life.
- ✔ There are no guarantees that your earnings will always rise.
- ✔ Men's biggest earnings come in their forties, for women it's in their thirties.
- ✔ Missing out on early promotions can have a big impact on your lifetime earnings.
- ✔ If you missed out on promotion, you need to find other ways to boost your earning power.
- ✔ Every economic cycle provides opportunities to boost your income.

4.
Create wealth

E**ven though I've said** this is a book about making the most of what you've got and not necessarily about becoming wealthy, I bet there are a few people who are secretly hoping I'll just tell them how to become really, really rich. Well, I'm about to.

Aside from a lottery or pools win, or an inheritance from a wealthy distant relative you never knew you had, I only know of one way to get rich and it's this: you've got to create wealth. The best way I know to do this is by starting a business, but it's not the only way.

Starting a business

If you don't fit into a career pigeonhole, if you never got the right qualification, missed out on promotions or just don't fit in well with hierarchical structures, I believe that starting a business is the best way to achieve financial security. However, a successful business isn't automatically one that produces wealth.

Many small businesses provide their founders with a good income and hopefully a nice lifestyle, but when those founders retire, the business shuts its doors and is wound up. To create wealth, you have to build a business which is worth just as much – or more – without you at the helm. You can do this through expansion: if one shop makes £30,000 a year with you managing it, you could open another shop and pay a manager £20,000 a year. If you do this several times, you could stop working in the first shop and collect £10,000 profit from an army of shops rather than £30,000 from the one shop. Let's say you eventually have 10 shops and you put your business up for sale. Typically, businesses are sold for a multiple of profit, and in retail let's say it's six times the profit. As you have 10 shops making £10,000 each a year, that's a profit of £100,000, so you should be able to sell your business for £600,000. Congratulations – you just created a lot of wealth!

You can also create wealth by combining raw materials in such a way that they are more valuable than the sum of their parts. If you have the skill to take £5 of raw materials and combine them with £2 of labour to make a £10 product, then you have created value. If you can sell 100 of your products, you've made £300, but if you can sell a million of them, you've made yourself £3 million. Creating substantial wealth in business is about scale. Creating a *saleable* business means creating a *scaleable* business where the operation is so well set up that anyone could buy it and run it just as efficiently – if not more efficiently – than you do.

If you have an idea for a business, go for it. Whether or not it makes you wealthy, you will acquire skills that will enable you to earn a living no matter what happens to the economy and have commercial experience that will be valuable to any employer. If you want more advice on how to get your idea off the ground, pick up a copy of one of my other books, *Wake Up and Change Your Life,* which will take you through the start-up process step-by-step.

Commercial bonuses

We've all heard stories about stockbrokers and hedge fund managers who get multimillion-pound bonuses, and I'm sure most people can't believe that anyone can do anything so valuable that they deserve to get paid that much. Yet it has been financially viable for City institutions to pay those levels of bonuses, so how is that?

Well, it's because those traders have created wealth. If someone receives a bonus of £1 million, you can be pretty sure that the value their actions have added to their company's wealth exceeds £10 million. If a fund manager starts the year with a £100 million fund of money to invest and through knowledge and skill turns that fund into £110 million, why shouldn't he or she earn a 10% bonus and pocket a million?

Whether or not you think it's fair, the point is it's commercially sensible for companies to incentivise their staff to create wealth – what they pay out in bonuses is only a percentage of the profits they've made. Of course, you don't have to work for a bank or brokerage to get a big bonus. Some companies cherry-pick employees to set up new divisions, often in new territories, and incentivise them to make profits by giving them equity stakes in the new division. If you know a way that you can create wealth within a corporate structure, you owe it to yourself to work for a company that will pay you a percentage of the additional wealth you've created. Any decent manager will respond positively to a suggestion for wealth creation from a keen member of staff, and any decent manager would be happy to incentivise that member of staff to deliver on their vision.

Investments

We'll come on to investments in detail later in the book, but I want to mention them here because they can enable you to create wealth. If you take the example of the investments I make in *Dragons' Den*, I put money into a small company that allows it to expand in return for a stake in the business. When that business grows, so does the value of my equity stake, so when I sell my shares I make a profit in excess of my original investment. Whether you are putting your money into a business venture, a property or a hedge fund, the same principle is adhered to: your investment allows wealth to be created and you make a profit.

The problem with investments is that they don't often come with guarantees. As an investor you accept that the opportunity to make money also means there is an opportunity to lose it. The opportunities that offer the biggest rewards are usually the ones that come with the biggest risks. Nevertheless, the world's richest man, Warren Buffett, isn't an entrepreneur, he's an investor. If you get your investment strategy right, you create the opportunity to amass a great deal of wealth.

Whichever method of creating wealth appeals to you, I hope you understand that wealth doesn't just happen organically; it requires effort and application. Unless you are happy with the 14 million:1 odds of winning the lottery, if you want to get wealthy you must accept that the way to do this is through work. Hard work. And lots of it. While this may not be what you want to hear, the good news is that the harder you work, the more you reduce the risk that your endeavours will fail, and the more wealth you are likely to create.

CHECKLIST

- ✔ **If you want to be rich you have to create wealth.**
- ✔ **The best way to do this is to start a business.**
- ✔ **The next best way to do this is to help your company create wealth.**
- ✔ **If you create wealth for a company, it's reasonable to expect a percentage of that wealth to be paid to you in the form of a bonus.**

PART THREE
Spending it

1.
The real value of assets

Being a smart spender can have almost as big an impact on your finances as being a smart earner. Generally, everything we buy falls into one of two camps – assets and objects. If you know which is which, then you can make smarter purchases.

An asset is something that has a value. The biggest asset most people have is their home, but cars, art, furniture, collectables – anything that can be exchanged for money – are also considered assets. Everything else is just an object .

Appreciation v depreciation

Because assets have a tradable value, the amount they are worth can change. Some assets are likely to increase in value – traditionally, property has been seen as a good bet – and some are pretty much certain to fall in value, like cars. The problem is that we can rarely be absolutely sure that something will appreciate in value – some cars are so collectable they increase in value, while property prices are affected by dips in the market – so we can never talk in absolutes about appreciation and depreciation. However, what we can do is acquire the ability to analyse our purchases more strategically.

The value of assets is mostly determined by the forces of supply and demand in conjunction with the desirability of the asset. If something is desirable and scarce, it will increase in value. If something is desirable yet readily available, then its value is unlikely to increase. If a product is undesirable –

last year's computer model, for example – then its value will decrease even if it's hard to find. An undesirable product that is widely available isn't really an asset at all, it's an object.

Let me give you the example of Harry Potter first editions. Book collectors pay tens of thousands of pounds for a first edition of the original Harry Potter book because only a few thousand were printed. The popularity of Harry Potter means that these rare first editions are likely to increase in value. Yet you can walk into a bookshop and buy a copy of *Harry Potter and the Philosopher's Stone* for under a tenner. So why is one copy of the book worth a fortune and the other just a few quid? It's that mix of desirability with supply and demand.

Yet you might look at this example and say, 'Why on earth would I spend £20,000 on something that I can buy for £6.99? How can that possibly be sensible?' I wouldn't disagree with you. The fact is that what's worth something to you may be worthless to someone else, and that's why assets don't have a finite value: an asset is only worth what someone will pay for it. The true value of anything is only determined when a willing seller sells whatever it is to a willing buyer.

Smart spending

The more often we spend our money on appreciating assets, then the smarter we are being with our money. However, the vast majority of our money is spent on objects. If you analyse where your money goes each week, it's probably spent on food, utilities, transport, going out, clothes and newspapers. We can't avoid these purchases and we accept that as soon as we pay for most of these items, they are virtually worthless. Even occasional purchases like fridges and sofas are worth a fraction of what we paid for them as soon as they are delivered, so the smart thing is to find purchases that will last longer so that they won't have to be replaced so often. If you buy a sofa for £299 you might think you've got a bargain, but if it only lasts for 18 months before the springs go, you could argue that it has cost you more than the £599 sofa that might have lasted a decade.

Smart spending isn't about *not* buying things, it's about buying them *carefully*. We will always have to spend on those daily, low-value items and we will occasionally have to buy the higher-value items like appliances and cars. What we need to try to do is balance that spending with the purchase of a few assets that will appreciate in value. Generally, the more expensive the item you buy, the more carefully you should consider whether it is an appreciating or a depreciating asset.

You can't avoid buying a car – or many other assets – that will drop in value (unless you get into classic collectors cars, of course) because a) cars become less reliable as they age and get dents and scratches that make them less desirable, and b) manufacturers bring out new models with better features. The new models virtually guarantee that the older models will lose their value even more rapidly. However, in these situations you still have a choice between a model which is likely to lose value quickly and one more likely to retain its value. We can also protect the value of our new asset by looking after the car so that it will hold more of its value than one which is poorly maintained.

The point is that some purchases are assets and deserve to have their value protected, and some purchases don't. Even though we can't always buy appreciating assets, we can often control – and slow – the rate at which an asset depreciates. Managing your assets can have a big long-term impact on your bank balance.

 **CHECKLIST**

- ✔ **Our spending can be broken down into two categories: assets and objects.**
- ✔ ***Objects* are virtually worthless once they've been bought; *assets* retain some of their value.**

✔ Some assets appreciate in value while others depreciate.

✔ Managing the rate at which our assets decline or increase in value has an impact on our wealth.

2.
Do you really need it?

If we all asked ourselves this question before we bought anything, the economy really would grind to a halt! While frivolous spending might keep the country's economy going, it can ruin yours. Now that most of us carry a couple of credit or debit cards in our wallet, it's just too easy to buy whatever we fancy without really considering if we actually need it, and this is why so many people have ended up in debt.

I suppose you could argue that we actually *need* very little; after all, across the world over a billion people survive on less than $1 a day. I don't think there can be any argument that in 21st-century Britain we all have extremely comfortable lives compared to people in developing countries who survive on one meal a day and where entire families share a single room with their cow and their duck. However, I don't think it's unreasonable to say that we have more needs than just survival in modern Britain. The economics of the developed world mean that a much higher basic income is required and that certain purchases are necessary to maintain a basic standard of living.

These are the basics that I think should be the financial priority for every household:

- A roof over our heads
- Utilities: electricity, water and, I'd argue, a phone
- Food
- Clothing
- Medicines
- Transport

Your list might be slightly different, but I think if we can afford everything on that list we can say our basic *needs* have been met. Yet our lifestyles demand so much more expenditure that it's difficult to determine when our spending is purposeful and when it starts being reckless. Identifying that boundary between purpose and recklessness and being very careful about how often you cross that line means you are unlikely to get into trouble with your spending.

The more we have, the more we need

Have you ever heard people say that the reason why computers are becoming so cheap is because the real money is made in selling us the software? Or that there's more money to be made in selling photocopier cartridges than there is in selling the photocopiers themselves? It seems to me that whenever we make one purchase, we have to make another to maintain the initial purchase.

We become trapped in a cycle of spending and it's hard to know what we need any more. Let's say you get a new job that pays £4,000 more than your current job. You would assume that you would be better off, wouldn't you? But what if it costs £1,000 a year to commute to that job, and the cost of buying lunch each day works out at £20 a week, and that because it's a more senior position you are expected to wear smarter clothes, and of course it would really create the wrong impression if you didn't wear different clothes to the office each day. With all that spending, are you still better off? On the basis that to get on in our commercial world you need to adhere to certain social norms – washing regularly, using deodorant, buying the odd round in the pub after work! I think you can argue that we actually *need* a lot more than the basics.

I think this is part of the reason why so many people get into trouble with store cards and credit cards, running up huge debts to pay for things because they can't quite tell if they need them or not. After all, if you need a good pair of shoes to go to work in, how can you judge that you don't actually need a second pair?

In every area of our life, things that aren't essential for survival have acquired 'must-have' status. Does the guy who works in finance really need a satellite TV subscription so that he can watch Bloomberg? You could argue that even if he doesn't need it, it's certainly a legitimate bit of expenditure because keeping up to date on the financial news may benefit his career. Equally, does the woman who uses her car to drive to work really need breakdown cover? Maybe not, but maybe it's only because she's got breakdown cover that she feels confident taking on the journey in an old banger that's cheaper to keep on the road than a newer car.

Is it appropriate?

Given that our financial commitments are so intertwined with our lifestyle and it can be so easy to justify high levels of expenditure, how do we make sure that we're not wasting our money buying things we don't really need?

I don't think it's reasonable to say that in this day and age, the answer is to deny ourselves everything – we need a way of distinguishing our reckless spending from our purposeful spending. My solution is to ask another question: is it appropriate?

Let's take that second pair of shoes to wear to work. Is it an appropriate purchase? In the case of a worker whose income allows for a lot of discretionary spending, the answer is 'yes', but for someone whose budget is a lot tighter, is it still appropriate? If the second pair of shoes allows them to walk into their place of work with more confidence, if the money spent on the shoes isn't at the expense of the items on my essentials list and if the shoes are well made and reasonably priced, then I would say it is appropriate. But if the shoes are unsuitable for the workplace, if similar shoes are available elsewhere at a cheaper price, then I think you could say that it would be inappropriate to buy them.

I think we all know deep down if a purchase is appropriate or not. I think we are capable of deciding if it's appropriate to pay for a satellite TV subscription or not in our particular circumstances. However, in the recent past, we have collectively fooled ourselves into thinking that what we want is what we need.

While there are some expenses it's becoming harder and harder to avoid calling essential, it's also becoming easier to spend money thoughtlessly. The fact that we rarely count the cash out when we pay for something over the counter, or that the direct debits leave our account without our knowledge, means it's very easy to pay for things we don't really need. For instance, if you book a holiday, it's quite likely that you will be offered insurance against cancellation and as it's easier to say 'yes' rather than shop around for a better deal, lots of people end up paying for insurance they don't really need. It's not that I'm advocating that you should travel without insurance, it's that you might already be covered by another policy – perhaps an annual travel policy, your employer's insurance, your home insurance or a freebie you get from your credit-card provider.

I recently went to buy a camera in Curry's and the sales assistant told me that the memory card it came with only held four photos, so I really ought to buy a second one. I agreed. A decent case for the camera was also a good idea, he suggested, and I agreed. As I was going to be using it in Africa where charging up batteries isn't always easy, he suggested I also get a second battery pack, which took the price to £540. However, he then told me that the battery pack wasn't in stock: they could get it for me but there would be an £8 delivery charge! I stared at him – he was serious. 'You really think it's okay to charge your customer for getting your stock delivered?' He said it was company policy. I decided there and then that while I could justify all the other expense, that £8 was unjustifiable and therefore wholly inappropriate and I left without buying any of it. (In the end, I actually ended up buying the same camera package at the airport for £420.)

Unless you ask yourself if each and every purchase is appropriate, it's just so easy to end up spending a lot of money inappropriately.

Take an inventory

Things you will never benefit from are clearly things you don't need, so I suggest that you take an inventory of all your expenditure. Go through your bills, bank statements and the budget you prepared earlier on and see if there's anything you're paying for that you really don't need. Some of the things you could be looking out for include:

- An inclusive phone package that works out more expensive than paying for individual calls.
- Insurance for something that you no longer have.
- An insurance policy that is now invalid because your lifestyle has changed.
- Insurance for something that is also covered under another policy.
- A direct debit for a service you no longer use.

Look at your receipts for the past few months and ask yourself how appropriate your spending has been. Can you see patterns in your spending where you're buying more than you should have? Now ask yourself this: would you rather still have that money in the bank instead of having spent it frivolously? If the answer's yes, you're on your way to being a lot smarter with your money.

CHECKLIST

✔ Work out if you need something, or if you just want it.

✔ Identify whether a purchase is purposeful or reckless, and
   if you can't, ask yourself if it's *appropriate*.

✔ Carry out an inventory of your current spending to see
   where you are spending money unnecessarily.

3.
What's it really worth?

After buying stuff we don't really need, the next most common mistake we make with our purchases is paying too much for them. For me, one of the cornerstones of being smart with money is never paying over the odds.

In the previous chapter, I talked about how much more a first edition of a Harry Potter book sells for than the latest edition available on the high street. When two near-identical items vary so much in value, it can be very hard to work out just how much an item is really worth. I'm sure we're all familiar with those features in fashion magazines where there's a picture of a celebrity in designer clothes next to a model in the high-street equivalent of the same outfit. The celebrity's wardrobe comes with a price tag in the thousands (even though the celebrity was probably given the clothes for free from the designer), yet the high-street version comes in at under £100. How can two virtually identical outfits be worth such differing amounts?

Being able to work out what something is really worth prevents you from paying celebrity prices for high-street products.

Compare prices

The first way to assess the value of something is to compare its price with a similar or identical product elsewhere on the market. The internet makes this a doddle, and whether you want to buy a second-hand computer, a brand-new car or, a frying pan or a Banksy original, it won't take you long to see what the going rate really is.

There are several price comparison sites (e.g. pricerunner. co.uk, kelkoo.co.uk) where you can key in the model number of the item you're interested in and they will tell you the prices several retailers will charge you for it. If you're buying a car, the specialist site www.parkers.co.uk gives standard valuations of most common makes of cars.

For more unusual items, I find that eBay – of which I'm a really big fan – can quickly determine how much something is really worth. Search for similar items and follow the auctions without bidding to see how much items go for. That way, when you bid for something, you can make sure you don't pay too much.

Research really is the best way to find out an item's true value. Whether you're getting a quote from a plumber or hiring a car, the only way you can check you're not being overcharged is by shopping around. I never take the first offer I am made – I always get a second quote and usually a third. And I make sure everyone who gives me a quote knows I will be talking to other providers as that way they're more likely to give me a competitive price.

Often, salespeople will try to get you to make a quick decision by saying something like 'If you pay now I'll give you a discount'. In my experience, if they can give you a discount today, they'll be able to offer the same discount in a couple of days' time – don't let yourself be pressurised into buying something that you're not sure of the value of. Once I've got a range of quotes, I phone the company that I liked the most and want to do business with and say something like: 'The price you've given me is more than I've had from your rival Acme Trading. I wanted to give you the chance to beat their quote.' People hate losing out to their rivals, and taking your business away from someone else is often worth taking a percentage off their original quote. The more you talk to people, the closer you will come to the true value of the item.

The cash:time ratio

One of the most common forms of overspending is paying people to do things we can do more cheaply ourselves. While some jobs will always need experts, others like painting and decorating, servicing a car or even booking a holiday don't, yet these are all tasks we frequently hand over to professionals or agents.

The way to work out if their services are worth paying for is to work out how long it would take you to do their job. Let's say you get a quote from a decorator to paint the outside of your property for £550, made up of £100 for materials and £450 for the labour. You need to ask yourself two questions: how long would it take you to do the job yourself and how long would it take you to earn £450?

If it would take you three days, that means it would cost £150 a day. If your net earnings are more than £150 a day, paying the decorator probably makes sense. If you earn less than this, what's the point of working four or five days to earn the money to pay for a three-day job? And this is assuming you can't do it on your days off.

When you're working out the cost of services that you could do yourself – unblocking drains, simple DIY, curtain-making – you have to factor in the time taken to do the job against the time needed to earn the money to pay for the job.

Negotiating

The best way to work out the price you should pay for anything is by negotiation. Even high-street shops that appear to sell items for set prices can be surprisingly negotiable. I understand that a lot of people are a bit shy about negotiating; I think it's because they feel that they are hurting the person they want to barter with by reducing their profit. The truth is there are very few win/lose negotiations in life and negotiation is usually just a process that allows both parties to get what they want out of a situation. That shop manager you think will hate you if you ask for a discount would probably rather give it to you than have you leave the premises without making a purchase.

The first thing to get right with a negotiation is the tone. If you demand a 20% discount, the thing you can be sure of is that you will get the other person's back up. I find saying something like 'Can you help me out here? If you can knock something off then I might be able to buy it,' is much a better way to start the conversation.

It's also usually best to get them to come up with a new price because if you just ask for 20%, you won't be uncovering information – and information is how you will establish the item's true value. There'll be a reason why they are willing to accept a discount – maybe it's the trading conditions, maybe it's because they hope you will become a regular customer, it might be because it's an end-of-line item or it's the end of their accounting period. When you know why they are prepared to discount, you get a clearer picture of how much something is worth.

In any negotiation you should always know what the deal is worth to you. You should decide the maximum price you're willing to pay (or if you're selling, below). If your negotiation so far hasn't dropped to the level you are happy with, you can then make them an offer of the price you want to pay and they can choose whether or not to accept it. For this to be a success-ful strategy, you have to be prepared to walk away.

What's it worth to you?

Price isn't the only consideration when making a purchase. The item has a monetary value, but so does the level of cus-tomer service you get, the speed with which you can have the item, not to mention the quality of the item itself. A speedy plumber is worth more than a slow one, a coat that lasts for two winters is worth more than one that won't make it to January and a guarantee that offers peace of mind is worth paying a premium above the value of the goods or services being bought or exchanged.

And for some people, a first edition Harry Potter is worth a thousand times more than other people would pay for the same book. That's because the value of items is affected by a range of forces – the desirability of the item, its availability, its condition – all of which make the first edition very valuable because there is an established market for rare books. However, sometimes an item might be desirable, hard to get hold of and in mint condition, but the lack of an established resale market means that it isn't as valuable.

This is why working out how much something is worth to you is just as important as investigating comparisons. Let's take the example of designer clothes. There's no doubt that designer clothes are usually better made and use better materials, but this alone doesn't account for the inflated cost. There is a premium for the fashion label itself, and this has an intangible value for some people. There are all sorts of reasons why we might pay over the odds for something, but they pretty much all boil down to the way our purchase makes us feel. If we get a kick out of wearing designer clothes, then we justify the expense, just as some people like the feeling of owning their own set of golf clubs rather than hiring a set from the clubhouse. It might be that they really do feel better in the expensive clothes, or play better with their own clubs, and therefore the cost that most of us would find unnecessary is one they will happily pay.

The key thing with assessing what anything is really worth is to ask yourself the question I've been telling you to ask of everyone else: what do *you* get out of it?

CHECKLIST

✔ You establish something's true worth by comparing prices and negotiating.

✔ The cash:time ratio means it's cheaper to do some jobs yourself.

✔ What something is worth can depend not only on value but convenience and prestige.

4.
Get your spending under control

I've talked a lot so far about taking responsibility for your finances, and while people are usually keen to get on top of their earnings and maximise their income, keeping on top of their spending seems like a chore. I've said all along that being smart with money means balancing five key areas of our financial life – earning, spending, borrowing, saving and investing – so taking control of your finances means keeping track of your spending.

Let me make one thing clear: this chapter is not about denying yourself anything, but if you are on a limited budget or are trying to get yourself out of debt, the advice here will be a big help towards getting your finances sorted. I understand how easy it is to get to the end of the month and wonder where the cash went. When the credit card bill arrives, there are usually a couple of transactions you've forgotten about, and when you look at your bank statement, there are always more debits than you'd expected. Now that we can get cash out whenever we want and can pay for everything from a round of drinks to a newspaper with plastic, it's easy to let spending get out of control. If you take on board some of these ideas, your credit card bill and bank statement should stop springing quite so many surprises on you.

Make a note of it

A friend of mine has four children, and at least once a day one of the kids will say, 'Mum, can I have . . .' She got bored of saying 'No' – and she didn't like saying 'No' – so she started asking her kids to make a note of the thing they wanted, and if they still wanted it when their birthday or Christmas came round, then she would buy it for them. It stopped the pestering and the kids didn't get stroppy because they weren't being told 'No' all the time. When the kids' birthdays approach, she goes through the lists the kids have made and do you know the remarkable thing? At least half the items on the list aren't wanted any more. Making a note of the things you want to buy is a really good way of making sure that you don't spend your money on things you'll quickly discover you can live without.

I'm not suggesting that you only buy things at birthdays and Christmas, but perhaps leaving things for a month is a pretty good idea. If you make a note of everything you want and then decide at the end of the month what you want the most, you're unlikely to overspend.

What's in your wallet?

How many cards do you carry around with you? A debit card? A credit card? Maybe two? A card to get at your savings account? A store card? The more you have, the easier it is for your spending to run away with itself: if one card is refused, you can always pay with a different one. If you don't carry the means to pay for things, you are forced to give your purchases some thought: if you had to return the next day with the method of payment, I bet your spending would plummet. Of course, that's not practical, but limiting what we carry around with us, perhaps just one credit card and one debit card, would mean that you at least couldn't spend more than your limit.

If you know you've got into some bad spending habits, why not go a step further and only carry cash for a couple of weeks and see what a difference it makes. Counting out the notes and handing actual money over the counter makes you realise that *buying* something actually *costs* something.

Casual spending

Just like we could all find more time to do the things we really care about if we watched a little less TV, we could all find a little more money in our pockets at the end of the month if we could just stop ourselves from buying coffees, newspapers, lottery tickets and thousands of other things we pick up without thinking. When something costs less than a couple of quid, how can buying it really affect your overall financial health? By buying lots of them!

Incidental spending can really mount up. Do you realise that the £1.79 cappuccino you buy at the station each morning works out at £8.95 a week? Which means you're spending around £450 a year on coffee! This is okay if you intend to spend £450 on coffee, but if you don't even notice you're spending it, I think giving yourself a budget will mean you've got more money left for the things that really matter.

Once your essentials – rent, bills, food, travel etc – are paid for, calculate how much you've got left each month. Now decide how much of that sum you're willing never to see again and make that your monthly budget. If you're a problem spender, I would suggest that most days you don't take any cards out with you and instead get out your weekly allowance in cash each Monday. That way when it's spent, you can't spend any more.

Keep a record of your spending

For a couple of months – even just a couple of weeks would help – have a go at keeping a record of everything you spend money on. Not only will this help you see how quickly you're eating into your monthly budget, but it will almost certainly reveal where your spending is under control and where you lose control. Most of us have a weak spot in our spending – computer games, betting, shoes, downloading music, cake –

and keeping a record is the best way I know to identify the areas of your financial life where you throw caution to the wind.

There are lots of areas in our life where our spending can remain hidden from our consciousness – popping out for lunch with co-workers, picking up emergency supplies from the corner shop, giving pocket money to the kids – and it's only a written record that can help you bring these hidden expenses into the light. Possibly the easiest way to forget you've bought something is when you shop online. It's one thing when you pay for something in a shop with a piece of plastic, but when the item you're buying is only real once it's delivered, it can feel that your spending has little to do with your financial reality.

Why are you buying it?

There have been plenty of reports over the years that have concluded that we often buy ourselves 'treats' to 'reward' ourselves. These same reports tell us that some people really do get a buzz out of shopping in a way that others get a thrill out of watching football or drinking alcohol. The lift they get when they buy something new has been proven to be addictive.

If you think you might have a serious problem with spending, perhaps you could ask yourself why you really feel compelled to buy things. Is there some area of your life that's causing you so much stress that you need to buy things just to make yourself feel better? Perhaps the spending isn't the problem, maybe it's something else in your life and if you got that sorted, you might feel better able to resist buying so much stuff.

CHECKLIST

✔ Set a budget for your casual spending.

✔ Make a note of the things you would like to buy: once a month look at your wishlist and prioritise your spending.

✔ Only take out as much cash as you've budgeted for the week – when it runs out, you have to stop spending.

✔ Keep a record of your spending so you can fully appreciate your spending habits.

5.
Lifetime spending

Earlier in the book, we looked at lifetime earnings and how there are predictable peaks and troughs in our income. It's not a big surprise, then, that there are also times in our life when our spending exceeds others. Anticipating when you are likely to incur increased costs is the first step on the way to making sure you'll be able to afford them when they come along.

Here's a graph of what I reckon is the spending graph of a typical Briton:

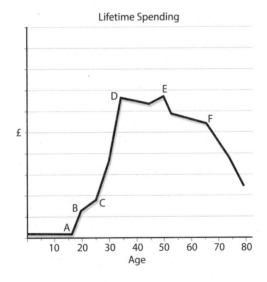

It doesn't take a genius to guess what's happening to this person's spending at the milestones in their life. At point A, they're probably a student living cheaply in a flatshare. At point B, they've started to live by themselves and are incurring the extra expense of solo living. At C, they start a family and their expenditure rockets. At D, there's a period of consolidation after the flurry of home improvements and child-rearing costs that ballooned in their thirties, but at E, the kids are at university and need financial assistance. At F, the mortgage is paid off and the outgoings slow down considerably as the children become financially independent, and spending continues to slow.

Give or take a few years, I bet this is the spending curve for millions of people, and even if yours doesn't follow this template, you'll have times in your life when there are greater demands on your financial reserves. Obviously, if you don't buy your own home, you won't have the expense in your twenties and thirties that's on this graph, but neither will your expenditure tail off once your mortgage is paid off.

Anticipation

If you can anticipate when you are going to need more money, you can make smarter decisions that will help you ensure you've got the right amount of cash when you need it. Give some thought now to the sorts of events in your life that will require more funds:

- Paying for your education.
- Saving up for a deposit to buy your first home.
- Increasing your mortgage payments to pay for a bigger home.
- Children.
- Helping your kids through university and maybe helping them buy a home.

There might be other things that you're looking forward to spending money on later in your life. If you know you want to buy a yacht when you retire, anticipating that cost means you can budget for it and earn the money to pay for it while you've got the chance.

Children

We all know that raising kids costs money, but it seems to me it gets more expensive every year. I've got six of them, so I know how the costs sneak up and then mount up. I'm not just talking about buying buggies, cots and nappies. For most people, starting a family means moving to a bigger and more expensive home, so before you've even bought anything for the baby, your expenditure has already taken a sharp upwards turn.

Then there's the cost of childcare (although there is government help towards this in the form of tax credits if your household income is below £58,000), and when they're older you'll be shelling out for school uniforms, travelling to school and back, after-school clubs, packed lunches, school trips . . . the list could fill the rest of this book. Research by the insurance company Liverpool Victoria in 2008 put a colossal figure on raising a child from birth to the age of 21 – £186,000! And that doesn't include school fees. You can add on another £73,000 if you want to send your child to a private school. It was knowing that I wanted to start a family and give my kids a good life that gave me the motivation to start a business and create some wealth. I really don't know how we'd have managed if I hadn't.

As with all statistics, you can play around with these figures until they stop making sense. If you don't pay for childcare or your child doesn't go to university, then the cost drops by almost half, but raising a child still takes an awful lot of money. And that's just one child. While 'economies of scale' mean the second child isn't quite as expensive as the first one, the bigger your family, the bigger your bills.

Planning

If you were to overlay your personal spending curve on top of your personal earning curve, you can start to see the times in your life when you need to save and when you can splash out. If your earnings rise in your twenties before your spending soars in your thirties, you've got a choice: spend it while you've got it, or put it aside for when you'll need it. It's your call, but at least now you've got the information to make an informed decision. You might feel that the surplus is better spent taking risks you might not be able to take when you have responsibilities, or you might prefer to be a sensible saver.

Similarly, if you can see that you are currently in a period where your expenditure exceeds your income but you can anticipate that either your spending will slow or your income will increase, you know you won't always be in debt.

If you anticipate a spending spike in the next few years, now is the time to plan how you will pay for the extra expenditure, either by making sure you increase your salary or by boosting your income in other ways.

Knowing when you can take risks with your money – whether with investments, frivolous spending or maybe starting a business – prevents the downside from being catastrophic. And as we'll see when we come on to borrowing and investing, assessing the risk is the foundation of clear-headed decision making.

 **CHECKLIST**

- ✔ Our spending fluctuates throughout our lifetime.
- ✔ Anticipating periods of greater spending means you can pay for them more easily.
- ✔ Knowing when your expenditure will rise and fall allows you to time your financial decisions more astutely.

6.
The best way to buy a car

After our homes, cars are often the most expensive thing we'll ever buy. If you buy a car the right way, you're not just saving yourself a couple of quid, you're saving thousands, and if you get it wrong, it can cost you dearly. Cars are a luxury for some but a necessity for most of us – particularly outside of urban centres – so I'd like to spend a bit of time explaining the best way to buy a car.

It's very easy to buy a better – and more expensive – car than you really need. Dealers are trained to make us add on optional extras and we end up with a nicer or bigger car than we meant to. If the purchase cost is your major concern, buy the smallest car that suits your needs, and don't worry too much about paying for optional toys. Keep in mind that any extras should always be in proportion to the make and model – for example, paying for leather seats in a Fiat Punto would be a waste of money, yet if you don't have them in an Audi TT, you might have trouble selling it.

Ongoing expenses

Once you've paid for a car, you start to incur other expenses. If you've borrowed to buy it, you'll obviously have a loan to repay, but even if you paid cash there are still a host of on-going bills, so when you are working out if you can afford to *buy* a car, you also need to calculate if you can *run* it.

If you have a poor driving history, are young and male or drive a powerful car, the cost of car insurance will be much higher than it would be for a 40-year-old woman with a clean licence. Of course, the level of cover you take out and the company you buy your insurance from can also make a big difference, so the first thing to do is log on to one of the countless insurance comparison websites and see if you could be paying less.

While buying a second-hand car is cheaper to purchase, the ongoing maintenance costs could make it more expensive to keep on the road. Classic and prestige cars aren't just expensive to buy, they cost more to insure and can be difficult to repair. No matter what you drive, you'll also have road tax to pay. It seems likely that cars with bigger engines are increasingly going to have to pay more in tax, so buying a smaller car can keep this cost down. It's also possible that you'll have to pay for a resident's parking permit, maybe parking at work, possible road tolls and congestion charges, not to mention petrol. Yet these aren't the biggest costs of owning a car . . . .

Depreciation

Except in a tiny minority of cases, cars are depreciating assets. Depreciation is the hidden cost of owning a car and the sad fact is that as soon as you buy a car it will be worth less than you paid for it. This is the real cost you need to factor into owning a car if you want to be smart with your money.

You pay a premium for buying a new car because as soon as you drive it off the forecourt it becomes a second-hand car: no one else can have that car new. Some of the mass-market models lose half their value in the first three years, regardless of the mileage on the clock, the optional extras or how well you've looked after it. If you bought a car brand new for £10,000, you'd be lucky if you sold it for half that just three years later. For a lot of people, this £5,000 will be more than the combined total of insurance, maintenance, petrol and parking they've paid out over those three years. The steepest depreciation happens in the first year and beyond three years, the rate at which a car depreciates can be minimised by the mileage and the condition, but it's only really collectable cars that stand a chance of holding their value in the long term – and only then if they are lovingly garaged and maintained.

It therefore makes sense to buy a car that's a couple of years old, and as some models depreciate faster than others, the smart thing is to buy a make and model that will depreciate as slowly as possible. Generally speaking, the makes that do well over time are BMW, VW, Audi and cars from other top-end manufacturers. The other thing that affects price, believe it or not, is colour. It might be boring, but black, blue, silver and red cars will do better over time than orange, lilac and banana yellow cars and there's a very good reason for this: they appeal to more people. And the bigger your market, the more you can charge. You can check out the devaluation costs of specific makes and models at www.parkers.co.uk.

Finance

Choosing the right way to pay for a car can affect how much it actually costs you. Many dealerships offer 0% finance on new models and there's a good reason for that – it's often the only way they can sell them! Seriously, because there's such a difference in price between brand-new and two-year-old cars, the only way they can shift them is if they make them easy to buy in instalments.

Generally, the better the finance deal, the faster the car is likely to depreciate in value, so don't be swayed by a low or non-existent interest rate if you don't really like the car. If the dealership's financial package isn't offering spectacularly low (or non-existent) interest rates, don't feel you have to finance the purchase through them. The chances are that if you check out the loans available from high-street banks, you'll find a cheaper deal.

Trade-ins

Most dealers will offer you money for your existing car, and the trade-in value of your current motor can play a big part in the price you pay for your new one. Confusing the value of your new car with the trade-in value of your current car is a technique dealers use to obscure the true value of the car they're selling you. If your current car is worth £1,000, it's not impossible that you might be offered £3,000 for it, which obviously seems like a good deal. But the truth is that if they'll give you more for your car than it's worth it's because they've got room to drop the price of the car they are selling you.

When buying a car, I always negotiate without revealing I have one to sell. I want to get the price down as far as I can and *then* I ask them what they'll give me for my current car. Letting them know too early that I have something to sell allows them to massage the figures. Although it's a hassle, you will probably always be better off selling your current car yourself through the small ads or eBay.

Do your research

Of course, the quickest way to lose money on a car is to buy a dud, and the fact that new cars come with guarantees is probably the most attractive thing about them. When you buy a second-hand car, you can check its history and make sure it's not the subject of an existing loan agreement, or has been in an accident or written off by a previous insurer. The AA carry out these checks, as do carcheck.com and hpi.co.uk: they cost about £20 and they could save you a fortune – and a big headache.

You can get a good idea of the price you should expect to pay by looking at car magazines and websites like whatcar. co.uk, autotrader.com and pistonheads.com. Once you've done your research, you might even feel confident enough to buy your next car at auction. There are some great bargains to be had at auctions, and if you've done your HPI checks you might get the car you want and at a price the high street will never give you. Of course, if you know a mechanic, ask for his advice as you could end up buying a huge repair bill if you don't know what to look for.

CHECKLIST

- ✔ You pay a premium for buying a brand-new car.
- ✔ As well as purchase costs, you need to calculate the running costs of a car.
- ✔ Depreciation is the hidden cost of buying a car – new cars lose half their value in the first three years.
- ✔ Avoid a seriously costly mistake by paying for an HPI check on any car you buy.

7.
Ways to pay

You might be surprised to hear that the way you pay for something affects how smart a purchase it is. Whatever it is you're buying, you usually have a choice in the method of payment, so I just want to quickly summarise the different options.

Cash

There aren't many businesses now that like to be paid in cash. A second-hand car dealership that might once have knocked a considerable sum off the selling price for a cash payment now has to deal with much closer scrutiny from the authorities and cash can often mean hassle; in fact, money-laundering laws *prevent* them from taking large sums of cash. A high-cash business is a target for thieves (and light-fingered staff – a term insurers call 'slippage' because money seems to 'slip' down the drain!) and incurs costs to do with holding cash, like using Securicor rather than simply transferring money electronically. These days, it's only when you're buying small purchases from small businesses that cash has significant bargaining power. For example, an electrician who's just carried out a small repair might take £30 cash rather than a cheque for £35, but it's now pretty rare that there's much difference between the cash price and the price by any other form of payment.

Although cash doesn't give you greater bargaining power, it can help with your budgeting. If you take out your weekly spending allowance in cash and then leave your cards at home, there's no way you can bust your budget. For me, that's the real value of cash these days.

Debit card

Payments from debit cards come straight out of your current account. You are not normally charged for using your debit card, so it can be a smart way to pay. However, there are a couple of drawbacks.

You might think that your bank won't authorise a payment unless you have sufficient money in your account to cover the transaction, but unless your account is seriously in the red, the chances are that the payment will go ahead, even if it means you go overdrawn, or worse, exceed your agreed overdraft limit, which means not just paying interest on your purchases, but a penalty 'unauthorised overdraft' fee too.

Debit cards are very convenient, but because they connect to your bank account, they are frequently targeted by fraudsters. If you think an establishment is a bit shady, don't use a debit card to buy from them, and make sure no one is looking over your shoulder when you tap in your PIN. Although banks generally reimburse money fraudulently taken from your account, it can take time and may mean you don't have sufficient funds to pay for your direct debits until you're reimbursed.

However, the advantage of debit cards is that once something is bought, it's also paid for, which means you won't get a shock each month when your credit card bill arrives.

Credit cards

I pay for pretty much everything on my credit card because they offer four notable advantages – as well as one enormous drawback. Let's start with the advantages:

1. You are not charged a transaction fee for using them (except, usually, on cash withdrawals and using them abroad);

2. Many card issuers insure the items you buy with your card so if anything happens to it before you get it home, you know you're covered. This is particularly beneficial if you are buying airline tickets: if your travel company goes bust, you will get your money back. When my fellow Dragons Theo Paphitis and Peter Jones took over a company that had gone bust that organised special adventures and day trips called Red Letter Days, customers who had paid by credit card received compensation from their card company while everyone else had to seek payment via the administration process. Unlike debit cards, if fraudsters clone or steal your credit card, it's the credit card company's money they're stealing and changing your credit card afterwards is much easier than changing your bank account.

3. A lot of credit card companies also offer incentives – either cash back on purchases, air miles, Nectar points or special offers – which make them a really smart way to pay as you could shop your way to a free flight to Australia!

4. Most cards don't charge you interest from the date of the transaction; in fact, it's not usually until a couple of weeks after your statement arrives. So if you buy something at the beginning of March and your bill doesn't come until the beginning of April, you probably won't have to pay for it until the middle of April – which means your own money has been sitting in *your* account earning *you* interest while you shopped with the card company's money!

The one HUGE drawback? Interest. If you buy anything with credit you could end up paying more for it that if you paid by cash. And if you don't pay off your bill in full each month, the interest on credit cards can be eye-watering. I'll cover this in more detail in the section on borrowing (page 107), but for now my message is this: use credit cards, but don't let them use you.

Store cards

Store cards have one big advantage: when you take them out, you usually get a discount on your first purchase, or vouchers towards future purchases. The reason stores can afford to offer these discounts is because they make their money back on all future transactions. The interest charged by the retailer is usually at the top end of what credit card companies charge and some even charge interest from the date of your purchase. I think store cards are the daftest way to pay for your shopping unless you have the discipline to take the free offer and then cut the card up, which is what I do.

Pay weekly

There are several operators whose business model involves letting people pay weekly for things that they can't afford to buy otherwise. So instead of paying £200 for a new washing machine, you pay a fraction of that each week. These operators perform a useful service for people who can't afford goods otherwise, but you have to ask yourself what they are getting out of it. The answer is 'a lot of money'.

Typically, the cost of paying weekly is 29% interest a year, which means that instead of buying a washing machine for £200, you are paying £260 for it – and that's only if you pay it back over a year. Often these deals are for longer pay periods and it's not unusual for a £200 purchase to actually cost £300. The total amount payable on weekly payments can work out 50% more than you would pay in a single payment. Whenever you make a purchase, always ask the retailer to tell you the 'Total Amount Payable' so that you can compare the real cost of your new purchase with what's available elsewhere. The headline figure always sounds cheap, but these deals will cost you in the long run.

Buy now, pay later

Plenty of retailers offer this as a way of financing larger purchases, typically sofas and other household items. Often the adverts offer 'Pay nothing for a year, then 0% interest' and it seems too good to be true. Yet again, you have to ask yourself: what are they getting out of it? How can that possibly make financial sense for them? The short answer is it doesn't if you stick to the payment plan, which means they are hoping that you won't.

These deals are often offered on items that need to be delivered, so they can be sure they have your real address. At the time of purchase, you will be asked to fill in finance agreement forms where you consent to future payments being taken directly from your account. So far it doesn't seem too unreasonable, does it? After the period when no payment is due, usually a year, the first payment will be automatically taken out of your account. Still sounds okay. But if you miss a payment, you will probably wish you'd read the small print. Sometimes the penalties on these too-good-to-be-true finance packages are severe, perhaps charging a high interest rate on the entire price of the purchase from the date of purchase. Let's say that you buy a sofa for £1,000, and after the first year, you start three years' worth of payments at £27.77 a month but you miss a payment in your final year. They might be charging as much as 35% interest, and they will automatically hit you for payment not just for 35% of the final year's payments, but on all four years' payments – which could cost you more than the sofa did.

Like credit cards, these 'buy now, pay later' deals can really help cash-strapped consumers, but be very careful because some of them have a huge and painful sting in their tail.

Direct debit

It's no surprise to me that utility companies frequently offer a discount to customers who pay by direct debit. The members of my health clubs pay by direct debit and the fact that I know for sure that their subscriptions will come in each month without fail allows me to run a more efficient business and offer more competitive rates. Not only do I know that the money is coming in regularly, but I don't have any banking charges or the increased costs of using a security courier service, or credit card processing fees.

Signing direct debit mandates that allow companies to be paid directly by your bank can save you money. Paying for any service – insurance, breakdown cover, gym membership, TV subscription, magazine subscription – by direct debit can often get you a discount. If one isn't automatically offered, ask for the direct debit rate and you'll probably find it's cheaper.

Direct debit guarantees mean that you can stop direct debits at any time, but if cancelling puts you in arrears with any of your suppliers, it may automatically terminate your contract with them and allow them to seek payment through other means.

 **CHECKLIST**

- ✔ The method of payment you choose can actually affect how much you pay.
- ✔ Credit card incentives – like cashback and vouchers – usually come with penalties if you don't pay off your balance in full.
- ✔ If you pay in instalments, you will usually pay more in the end.

PART FOUR
Borrowing it

1.
Good debt, bad debt

know for a fact that I wouldn't be wealthy – that I couldn't have *become* wealthy – if I hadn't got myself into debt. Every entrepreneur I know has used debt to make a profit, and most of the people I know who live comfortably in retirement owe their financial security to the fact that they were once in debt in the form of a mortgage on their home.

Yet debt has a bad name. So often we only talk about debt when it involves the people who struggle with debt – in many cases the people whose lives have been blighted by it – and we've come to think of debt as something to be fearful of.

So why is it that debt can be good for some people and terrible for others? It's because there is a good and bad kind of debt to get into. Learning the difference between the different sorts of debt can change your financial life. Debt, like money itself, is a tool and if it's used correctly, it can actually *make* you money.

In a nutshell, I believe good debt is when you borrow money to invest and bad debt is when you borrow to spend. Let me explain . . .

Good debt

Seventy per cent of Britons live in their own homes, and the majority of their properties will have been bought with the help of a mortgage. People have been happy to get into debt to buy a home because, over time, the price of their property is likely to rise while the size of their mortgage remains the same (or reduces as repayments are made).

I'm going to keep this simple: let's say you buy a house for £250,000. You have a £50,000 deposit and borrow £200,000 as a mortgage. You sell that house 10 years later when it has risen in value to £300,000. You repay the bank the £200,000 mortgage and are left with £100,000, or a 100% return on the £50,000 you originally invested. Obviously, housing markets go up as well as down, but history tells us they almost always go up after a slump, so the chances are that borrowing money to buy property will enable you to make money.

But it could be even more profitable than that. After 10 years of paying off the mortgage, you might have repaid as much as £80,000 of the £200,000 loan. So instead of giving the bank back £200,000, you only hand over £120,000, keeping £180,000 of the sale price for yourself. Even if the property doesn't increase in value in the 10 years you own it, you are still repaying the debt which is why so many people strive to own their own home rather than rent. We'll come on to what happens if the property has decreased in value in the chapter on Property.

Borrowing to invest is a tried and tested way of making money. Early on in my career when I was building a nursing home at the start of my care home business, I couldn't borrow the money I needed to complete the construction. After I sold everything I had, I took out £30,000 on credit cards – probably more like £100,000 in today's money – to pay the builders. People around me told me I was taking a huge risk, but I just didn't see it that way: I knew that as soon as the nursing home was built I could get a mortgage on it that would repay the card debts. I wasn't just investing in property, I was investing in my new business, and ultimately I was investing in me.

Professional investors talk about debt in terms of 'leveraging' where the potential gain exceeds the interest payable on the loan. A few years ago I completed a 'leveraged buy-out' when I borrowed money to buy a chain of health clubs. In business, we look for something called the Return on Capital Employed (ROCE) to assess an investment. In this case, the chain of health clubs cost me £90 million and produced £9 million a year in profits, which would have given me a return of 10%. But by leveraging the purchase, I boosted my ROCE because I used £20 million cash and a £70 million loan. I paid interest on the loan, which made my annual repayments £4.2 million, leaving me a profit of £4.8 million. So for my £20 million investment I was actually getting an ROCE of 24%.

Getting into debt allowed me to make a profit. If you can get your head round that, it's easy to understand why I think debt is a good thing.

Bad debt

Debt can be 'bad' for two main reasons. The first is borrowing to spend when, instead of investing in an appreciating asset, you buy items that decrease in value or – like holidays and entertainment – have no value. The advantage of borrowing to spend is that you can have what you want straight away, but the downside is that you will be charged interest on what you borrow. So let's say you borrow £1,000 to have a holiday from your bank at an interest rate of 11.79% to be paid back over a year. At the end of that year you will have paid your bank back the original £1,000 – what bankers called 'the principal' amount – plus £117.90 in interest. In other words, that holiday cost you £117.90 more than it needed to if you had paid for it without a loan. However, if you can afford the repayments, and you really enjoyed the holiday, it might be a price you are happy to pay.

The second reason that borrowing can be a bad idea – and this is far more serious – is if you cannot afford the repayments. If you took out a loan when you had a job, then lost your job and couldn't afford the repayments, the chances are that your lender would start proceedings against you to recover the 'principal' and any interest due. Ultimately, this could mean the bailiffs coming to your door to seize anything of value in your home. It's a pretty terrifying position to be in, and that's why getting into debt needs to be done with caution and forethought. Even debt secured against an appreciating asset can be a bad debt if you can't keep up the repayments.

There's one last thing that can affect whether a debt is good or bad, and that's inflation. Inflation is the rate at which prices increase each year, so if inflation is at 5%, what cost you £1 last year will cost you £1.05 this year. What this means is that your pound is worth less, so if you borrowed money last year, the amount you borrowed will have decreased in real terms, even though the actual figure won't have changed. Over time, inflation decreases the real value of the amount you owe, making it more affordable. Therefore, getting into debt in a period of high inflation can be seen as a good thing. The flipside of this, of course, is the effect *deflation* has on your money. If the rate of deflation is 5%, it means prices are falling and that the item which cost £100 will cost £95 this year. Long periods of deflation effectively increase the amount you owe. In a period of deflation, getting into debt costs you more than the interest rate you pay.

Gearing

When a business takes out a loan, the lender will want to know how heavily 'geared' the business is. Understanding why banks do this, and deciding on your own ideal gearing level, is a very good way of making sure that your good debts don't turn bad.

Gearing is the relationship between your assets and your debt. If you have assets of £100 and debts of £50, your gearing is at 50%. When businesses borrow, the bank may insist that their gearing doesn't fall below a certain rate to insulate them from any downturn in trade. The gearing rate is seen as so important by the banks that businesses are asked to sign a covenant to always keep their gearing within agreed limits, and if they break that covenant, the bank can ask for an immediate repayment of the loan.

The higher your gearing, the riskier your position and it's my bet that the companies that go bust during recessions are often those that have too high a gearing. So what should your personal level of gearing be? If you're young and have just taken out a 90% mortgage on your first home, your gearing rate is going to be very high, which means there isn't a cut and dried answer. Broadly, you want your gearing level to decrease as you get older so that you get to retirement with no debts (i.e. a gearing rate of 0%). If the bulk of your wealth is tied up in your property, house price gains will more than likely take your gearing level down automatically. If you don't own an appreciating asset, then you will only reduce your gearing by repaying your debts. I can't tell you what your gearing rate should be, but the lower it is, the more secure your financial position is.

 **CHECKLIST**

- ✔ Borrowing to invest is good debt.
- ✔ Borrowing to spend is bad debt.
- ✔ Paying interest on purchases makes them more expensive than the price tag.
- ✔ Debt allows you to leverage investments and get a better return on the capital you employ.
- ✔ Inflation reduces the value of the amount you borrow, while deflation increases it.
- ✔ Decide on an appropriate level of gearing and stick to it.

2.
Some debts are better than others

So far, we've talked about good and bad debt, and now we've covered the basics it's time to move on to talk about a sliding scale of debt from 'very good' to 'very bad'. An example of very good debt would be an unsecured loan on an appreciating asset at a very low interest rate. Leaving mortgages aside for the moment, the worst kind of debt is a loan secured against your assets, typically your property, that comes with a high interest rate and hefty arrangement fees. This chapter is all about identifying the kinds of debt available to you and choosing the right loan for the right purpose.

Remember when I said at the beginning of the book that one of the smartest things you can do in any transaction is ask yourself what they're getting out of it? The answers to that question might help you really understand how the debt industry operates. The thing to keep in mind is that banks don't like taking risks, and if you can provide them with a good credit history, some assets that the loan can be secured against, they will consider that lending to you involves very little risk. Low-risk borrowers tend to get very competitive interest rates. However, if you've got a poor credit history, or you can't offer any collateral for the loan, your lender is likely to want to reflect the risk they feel in lending to you by charging you a higher interest rate. It's the famous risk:reward ratio – the lower the risk you present to the lender, the lower the rate you'll have to pay.

Lenders are always looking to try to reduce the risk that they won't get their money back, and one of the ways they will do this is by trying to sell you something called Payments

Protection Insurance (PPI). For an additional monthly premium, PPI will cover your repayments if you can't afford to make them in certain circumstances (although overspending elsewhere certainly isn't one of them!). PPI has had a very bad press, and rightly so, as it was frequently mis-sold to people who wouldn't be able to claim (often the self-employed) or over-sold, giving borrowers the impression they could claim in situations that weren't covered. PPI is much better regulated now, but if someone tries to get you to take out a PPI policy with your loan, don't feel obliged. It's not a legal requirement but if you are interested in getting cover, do shop around, as you will almost certainly get a much better rate for PPI from another provider – the insurance *doesn't* have to come from your loan provider.

Secured and unsecured loans

When you approach a lender for a loan, you may well get offered two types of loan: secured and unsecured. A secured loan sounds better, doesn't it? Well, let me tell you, it isn't. Lenders will always try to secure the money they lend you against your assets. What this means is that if you default on your loan (i.e. if you miss some repayments), they will have a charge on those assets and they might be able to take them away from you. Lenders like to offer secured loans as it reduces their risk; in return, though, you usually pay a lower interest rate on a secured loan. However, it's pretty rare that the difference in rates between secured and unsecured loans is enough to make the risk of taking a secured loan worthwhile. Even if you think there's absolutely no chance that you will lose your job and will always be able to make your repayments, you might find out the hard way that life is full of surprises.

That said, there are some loans that will always require security. Mortgages, obviously, are loans secured against property. Many of the loans I have taken out in my career have also been secured against my home because the banks wanted to make sure I was incentivised to deliver on my business plan: a business owner who knows he might lose his children's home can be pretty much relied on to make sure his business remains solvent.

Interest rates and fees

Before I move on to discuss the various forms of lending, I just want to talk about interest rates. When you are looking to borrow, you should shop around for the cheapest loan in the same way you would shop around for the cheapest washing machine because the higher the interest, the more you have to pay. Good debt comes with the lowest possible interest rate. When rates are low, borrowing becomes more affordable, which means that low interest rates create an opportunity to boost ROCE levels. High interest rates may make some transactions unviable.

Just like kitchen appliances, you often get what you pay for. Loans are usually advertised with their interest rates, so the first thing you want to look for is the lowest possible interest rate available. But the lowest interest rate doesn't automatically mean the cheapest loan. Some lenders charge arrangement fees, which can be as much as 2% of the loan amount, while others have early redemption fees that mean you will incur a charge if your fortunes change and you want to pay the entire loan back early. It's not unheard of to also be charged a management fee, which basically means the lender takes another percentage for phoning you up every three months and asking if everything is all right. You also need to check whether the fees are added to the loan (in which case you will be paying interest on them) or are payable up front.

If you borrow £1,000 at an interest rate of 10% and pay it back over a year, your repayments will be roughly £91.66 (that's the loan amount of £1,000 plus £100 in interest divided by 12 months) and the Total Amount Payable (TAP) will be £1,100. If you pay it back over two years, your repayments will drop to £50 a month (that's the original £1,000 loan plus £100 in interest for each year of the loan divided by 12) but your TAP rises to £1,200. Increasing the repayment period reduces the repayments but increases the TAP.

If you have a choice of lender, go for one from an organisation you can trust, even if that means paying fractionally more for your loan. Should you get into difficulty with your repayments, dealing with a reputable firm will make your life a lot easier. However, you should keep in mind that the cheapest loans don't always come from the high-street lenders – the smaller lenders can't compete on visibility or marketing budgets, so they compete on deals. The best place to compare the best loans is in the 'best buy' charts in newspapers and sites like www.moneysupermarket.com.

Loans are offered at fixed and variable rates, and it's not always easy to work out which would work out cheaper in the long run. If you fix your interest for the life of the loan and interest rates go up, you'll be better off, but if they fall you will be kicking yourself. If rates are at a historically low level, then fixing is probably wise especially if knowing what your costs will be gives you peace of mind. You also need to check if the *repayments* will be fixed. As you repay the loan, your total debt reduces which means that your payments could in theory be reduced too, although it's standard for the repayments to remain at the original level because you pay the annual percentage rate (APR). If you pay the monthly rate, your repayments will start higher than they would be on the APR, but fall below the APR towards the end of the loan. Ask what the TAP would be to work out which works out cheaper over the life of the loan.

It's also worth pointing out that if you find out you've been overcharged for your financial services, you should complain, first to your bank and if that doesn't work, to the Financial Services Authority. In my experience those people who are prepared to bang on a few doors and create a bit of noise find their charges get reduced or waived. (It's the same with parking tickets by the way. If you complain about a borderline ticket, there's a reasonably good chance the ticket will be with-drawn.).

Questions to ask any lender

No matter who you are borrowing from or what you are borrowing for, the best way to check you're taking out the right loan for the right purpose is to ask a few questions. Don't sign anything until you've been given the answer to the following:

- Is the rate fixed or variable?
- Are the repayments fixed?
- Are there penalties for early repayment?
- What would happen if I missed a payment?
- Do you require any security?
- What is the Total Amount Payable (TAP)?
- Who will I talk to if I have a problem – someone in a branch or in a call centre?

Credit cards

I've already talked a bit about credit cards, so you'll know that I think they can be very useful. I pay off my credit card bill by direct debit each month so never get charged any interest and I never pay a fee. I also get 1% cash back on all my pur-chases, so every couple of months they credit money to my account. Giving me a card costs my credit company money, so they have to make their profit from their other customers. They make their money by charging late payers interest and by finding new ways to get you to spend their money.

Many card issuers have special introductory rates, often as low as 0%. As always, when something seems too good to be true, it usually is. Although the 0% rate makes a nice headline, the small print will no doubt reveal that the 0% only applies to purchases made with the credit card, not on cash advances. And if you transfer your balance from your old card to your new card, you're likely to be charged a percentage of the balance (usually between 2% and 5%).

When the interest-free period ends, you will generally go on to their standard rate and if you haven't cleared your balance before that happens, you will start paying a lot more than you need to.

Card issuers also sometimes issue you with cheques that you can use to pay for things you can't normally pay for with a credit card – for example, paying builders or paying off other loans. Before you use these cheques, take a look at the small print because you shouldn't assume that money spent with a cheque will be charged the same interest rate as money spent on your card – it can sometimes often be a lot more.

Credit card companies also charge for late payments – even during the introductory period – and if you don't pay off the entire balance each month, you will usually be charged interest on the entire balance, not just the remainder.

In my mind, credit cards are a good way of managing your cash in the short term, but a poor way to borrow money long term. You may be the kind of person who doesn't mind switching cards every three months to get the best rate, but given that the penalties for missing payments is so high, I think finding a card issuer who always has low fees and modest interest rates is a better long-term option.

Bank loans

Most people I know get a letter from their bank several times a year offering to lend them money. If you've got a decent banking history and a good credit rating (i.e. a track record for being solvent), banks would just love to lend you money and they don't care what you spend it on. They want you to have that holiday, or that car, or that night out right now, even more than you do.

Pretty obviously, the sensible thing to do is to save up for those things rather than paying for them in instalments with interest added to the bill. But, if you know you can afford the repayments, then taking out the odd loan isn't the most irresponsible thing you can do. After all, a well-timed holiday might be worth paying an extra few per cent for. The problem with loans is that you can get used to them and before you've paid one off, you've taken another out, and maybe another.

Constantly living beyond your means and making ends meet with loans is unhealthy as well as expensive. Debt is a major cause of depression, and while you might be able to juggle in the short term, very few people would tell you that living in debt in the long term is a good way to live your life. Difficult as it might be to accept, there are times when you can't really justify borrowing to spend. *Sometimes you just have to go without.*

Overdrafts

Most banks offer their customers an overdraft – an agreed figure that can be borrowed without applying for a loan – on their current account which can be very handy if you get paid late or have an unexpected expense. If your overdraft charges 15% interest and you dip into the red by £100 for three days, you will only pay a few pennies as the interest is calculated daily. If you didn't have an overdraft, your bank would probably charge you a much higher interest, but crucially you would also get stung with a penalty charge, which might be as much as £40. The problem comes if you aren't able to pay off the overdraft as that means you are paying a much higher rate than if you had taken out a bank loan (where the rates are usually about half the overdraft rate). Overdrafts are quick and convenient, but are only cost-effective for very short-term borrowing.

Some banks don't charge to arrange an overdraft (though when there's turbulence in the banking sector a fee isn't out of the question), and dipping into the overdraft reserve will only cost you the interest. If you go over your overdraft limit, however, you will usually get a penalty charge.

Student loans

I've said that good debt is when you borrow to invest, and borrowing to pay for your education through a student loan could be seen as investing in your future – and your potential earning power, as graduates tend to earn more than non-graduates. However, I think you need to be careful about the level of debt you take on as a student. The average student debt is now £17,500 (according to a survey in 2008 by the university website push.co.uk) and is likely to rise to over £20,000 for new students. Personally, I think that's a huge burden to start your career with.

So the first thing to ask yourself is how valuable do you think your degree will be? If you know what you want to do, might you be better off getting three or four years' worth of work experience under your belt rather than a qualification? If your chosen profession doesn't require professional qualifications, perhaps this is something you should consider. It might also be worth investigating whether or not you could study part-time or over four years rather than three, so that you can work part-time during your course and minimise your reliance on debt. Working in the holidays is another way of keeping your debts to a minimum.

In some professions, grants and sponsorship are available from the private sector and you should investigate every available source of income before you borrow. Your student status might also mean you can receive any income from employment without the tax being deducted at source – your university will have information on other income-boosting measures.

The most important thing is to live as cheaply as possible

while you're a student and thereby minimise your eventual debt – living in halls of residence, for example, rather than in private accommodation – and to work as much as is sensible to reduce the amount you have to borrow.

The good thing about student loans, compared to other debts, is that the amount you owe only attracts interest at the rate of inflation so the overall debt remains fixed in real terms. The other benefit is that you only start repaying the loan if your annual gross income is more than £15,000 when you start paying 9% of your earnings above that level. If you earn £16,000 a year, you'll pay £7 a month, and if you earn £35,000 a year, it works out at £150 a month. As loans go, it's a cheap form of debt, but it's still important to minimise how much debt you take on while you're studying.

Family and friends

Borrowing from friends and family can have some advantages over other sources of lending, the big one being that it is usually quick. No forms to fill in, no credit check, no five-day wait for the money to be available in your account. However, it usually comes with strings, and it's worth thinking about them before you ask your loved ones for money.

First of all, be absolutely clear if they expect interest to be paid on their loan. Secondly, establish a timescale for the loan to be repaid, and thirdly, make sure you both understand if the loan is to be paid back in instalments or in a lump sum. About 10 years ago, I lent someone in my family £12,000 and we actually wrote down the arrangement so we both knew where we stood. The loan was to be repaid at £100 a month with no interest payable *unless* a payment was missed. And do you know what? Every payment was made diligently until the full amount was paid back a decade later.

If someone is lending you the deposit to buy a flat, be absolutely sure whether they think they are receiving a stake in the value of the property, and what would happen if that stake became worth less than the original loan amount in the event of a house price slump. And if someone is lending you money to start a business, you need to discuss whether their money means they have any say in how the business is run or whether it entitles them to shares in the company.

Borrowing from people you know can be easy, but it can also be a nightmare. The problems usually arise when neither party talks about the details. If you know someone well enough to ask them for a loan, you should also know them well enough to talk through exactly how the loan will be repaid and what the consequences will be if it's not.

CHECKLIST

- ✔ Secured loans are generally cheaper, but they put your assets at risk.
- ✔ Check if you will be charged any fees for taking out a loan.
- ✔ Increasing the repayment period reduces the repayments but increases the total amount payable.
- ✔ Credit cards offer convenience and perks, but charge high interest rates.
- ✔ Overdrafts are cost-effective for small, short-term debts.

3.
Dealing with debt

Millions of Britons are in debt. Some know how they will pay their debts back, but quite a few are trapped in a cycle of taking out new loans to cover old ones or only paying the minimum amount each month, which means they are sinking deeper and deeper into debt. If you are struggling with your debts, there are several places you can go for help. Citizens Advice Bureaux (www.citizensadvice.org.uk, or look in Yellow Pages for your nearest branch) have a great reputation for helping people cope with debt problems, or you could approach the National Debtline (0808 808 4000) or the Consumer Credit Counselling Service (0800 138 1111). For what it's worth, here's my advice for getting back into the black.

Facing the problem

One of the reasons people get into debt is because they don't like talking about money, and unless that changes, every other step you take will get harder. The good news is that once you have faced the problem, things stand a chance of getting a lot better a lot sooner.

The first step is to add up all your debt – bank loans, credit cards, store cards, money owed to friends and family, overdrafts – and see just how much you owe (leave out your mortgage, if you have one). While you're going through this painful process, also make a note of the interest rate you are paying on each loan and how much your regular repayments add up to each month – this will help you decide how you repay each debt.

Dealing with the problem

Once you've been able to put a figure on your total debt, you're in a position to start working out how you can clear it. If your debt is modest, it may be enough to maximise your income and minimise your outgoings: the difference you save each month might be enough to start paying down your debts. But if your debts are substantial, you have to take more decisive action.

The first thing to do is to sort your debts into order of importance. Although the credit card companies will hassle you – perhaps even phoning you every day – they do not have the power to take your home away from you. And unlike the utility companies, they can't cut off an essential service. So prioritise by paying first the debts that put your home in jeopardy if you defaulted on them. When I was starting one of my early businesses, I had to do just this and opted not to pay one of my suppliers. When they sent me a lawyer's letter saying they were taking me to court I was actually relieved as I knew the legal process would take several months. In the meantime I could concentrate on meeting the demands of other creditors and keep a roof over my head.

If you've got to the stage where you doubt you will ever be able to repay your debts, it's time to talk to your lenders and see if you can negotiate your way out of the red instead. If your financial situation is temporary, they might agree a payment holiday or a reduced interest rate which will bring down your payments. Alternatively, they might extend the term of the loan which will also reduce your monthly payments.

If you don't talk to them and explain the problem, they can't help you. The less you explain why you have fallen behind, the more likely it is that they will start debt recovery proceedings against you. If you have been struggling for some time, it is possible that you can negotiate a final settlement with them. Let's say you owe a credit card company £2,000 and they are convinced that you will never be able to repay that debt, they might accept a lesser sum and cancel the rest of the debt. They would rather have, say £1,200, from you than nothing. You can negotiate these settlements yourself, or it can be something the debt counselling agencies get involved with. If you can negotiate final settlements with all your creditors, you can reduce your total debt significantly. All you need now is the money to make those settlements.

If you've been lucky with a windfall, this won't be a problem, but most people clear their troublesome debts by taking out a new loan. At the time of writing this book, the base rate was at 1%, the lowest rate in the history of the Bank of England. Traditionally, periods of low interest rates are a great time to sort out your debts: you can take out a loan at a low interest rate and use the money to pay off your old debts at higher interest rates. You are left with one lower monthly payment which should be much easier to manage. However, at the time of writing, while loans were cheap, the credit crunch meant they were also hard to get hold of.

'Debt consolidation' loans are frequently advertised as a magic solution to debt problems, which can even leave you with something left over for a treat. You would be a fool if you borrowed any more than you absolutely needed to: clear your debts first, then let yourself have a few treats. My advice is to avoid anyone that specifically targets people in debt: they probably devise their products and sales techniques with the knowledge that they will be dealing with customers who are vulnerable and possibly scared of finance. My hunch is that these specialist lenders won't give you the best re-financing deals and you would be better off talking to a traditional high-street lender.

CHECKLIST

- ✔ The first thing to do is to work out just how deep in debt you are.

- ✔ Prioritise paying the debts that are secured against your assets and home.

- ✔ If you will never have the funds to repay the debts, you may be able to negotiate paying off a smaller amount.

- ✔ Periods of low interest rates are traditionally good times to restructure your debts with cheaper loans.

PART FIVE

Saving and investing it

1.
Three good reasons to save

When **interest rates** on offer to savers are lower than inflation rates – especially when you take the tax off – and banks go bust taking their savers' money with them, as happened in 2008, it's not surprising that so many people feel that savers aren't rewarded. While people who have got into debt get support from government bailouts, people who have been responsible and put money to one side get slapped in the face. My feeling is that saving has its own rewards, and no matter what happens to interest rates, those who save a percentage of their income will always prosper. Yet 12% of Britons don't have any savings, and another 23% have less than £1,000 squirrelled away, according to the NS&I Savings Survey from 2007. That's 40% of the country with no safety net if their earnings unexpectedly dry up. I think that's pretty scary.

There are two reasons why people don't save: either they can't afford to or they just don't see the point. I hope that the first reason no longer applies to you as the changes I've talked about in this book mean you can end each month in the black, so I want to deal with the second reason. I understand that if you've only got £20 left at the end of the month, the temptation to have a nice night in the pub is pretty compelling, but even putting £20 away each month can make a difference.

When you're saving up for something specific, it's easier to put money away because you can see that you're getting closer to your goal. When I was saving up to buy my first house, I did shift work in a bakery and took all the work I was offered. It certainly wasn't because I enjoyed hauling trays of loaves around, it was because I got satisfaction knowing that a big slice of my earnings was going straight into my savings account. The fact that I was saving was a source of motivation for me and it enabled me to do a job I didn't enjoy with a smile on my face. The way I see it, there are three very good reasons to save.

Reason 1: Rainy days

How many times in the past year have you had to deal with an unexpected expense? Maybe your roof leaked, your car broke down or your washing machine packed up. I think it's pretty hard these days to go for a year without finding yourself shelling out for something you hadn't budgeted for. Having a rainy day fund means that these inevitable expenses will no longer cause you quite as much grief. And having the money handy means you won't have to borrow to pay for your emergency, which means you won't be paying unnecessary interest. In fact, you will be *earning* interest if you put your rainy day money into a savings account rather than a piggy bank.

Because the whole point of rainy day money is that you will need it at short notice, you'll need to keep it in an instant access savings account. This means you won't get the best rate of interest on it – you can get better rates if you are prepared to tie your savings up for a fixed period – but at least you won't have any penalties to pay when you need to get at your money.

Reason 2: A 'Sod You' fund

Having a bit of money in the bank gives you a certain amount of freedom and confidence, which gives you a psychological boost. Imagine having enough money in the bank to be able to say to your boss 'Sod you, I'm not taking it any more, I'm off!' Wouldn't that be great?

As a rough rule, a 'Sod You' fund (SYF) should be enough to keep you going for three months until you find another job, so to work out how much you should have in your fund, go back to your budget and see how much you'll need (bear in mind you might not be commuting during that period and other work-related expenses will shrink, so it might be a little less than you think).

Having three months' money in the bank removes a lot of the panic many people associate with financial choices. You don't have to feel pressurised into taking the first job you're offered, you can bargain harder in salary negotiations because you know you can walk away if you don't get what you want. Having a SYF means you don't fear the headlines in tomorrow's paper quite as much because it insulates you from the worst of what the economy can throw at you. Having a SYF fund makes life a hell of a lot easier.

Chances are that you won't need to get your hands on your SYF in an emergency. If you're leaving your job, you'll probably need to give notice, and if you're being made redundant, you'll probably get some kind of final payment. This means that you can put your SYF into a notice savings account that offers higher rates of interest, so long as you can give the bank or building society 30, 60 or 90 days' notice of your intention to make a withdrawal. Typically, the more notice you can give, the higher interest rate you will get.

Reason 3: It gives you options

Right at the beginning of this book, I talked about how individual pounds can't achieve very much, but if we club lots of pounds together they can start to make a difference, which is why giving small amounts to charities can make such a big impact. If you can learn to save, what you're effectively doing is clubbing together all of your loose pounds and letting them mount up until you can do something useful with them.

Spending money in dribs and drabs doesn't give you any real spending power, but collecting those dribs and drabs into a substantial savings pot can give you real bargaining power. In fact, it gives you financial muscle in every area of your life – if you want to start a business or buy your own home, savings are the tool that can help you get what you want.

Having a decent amount of money put by gives you options in life that you wouldn't otherwise have. For me, that's the most important reason to save. Frittering away money on pointless purchases doesn't create change in your life, but saving that money gives you the option to make changes if you want to.

If you aren't yet sure what you will use your savings for, you can keep them in fixed term savings accounts, which often give the highest interest rates. If you can tell a bank or building society that you won't be making a withdrawal for a year, two years, or maybe five years, they will offer you a substantially better return on your savings.

Wherever you keep your money, be aware of the current level of the protection offered by the Financial Services Compensation Scheme (www.fscs.org.uk). Currently, savers are guaranteed to get back the first £50,000 of their savings in each banking institution, so if you are smart enough to have saved more than the limit, make sure you spread your savings around so that you are fully protected if one of your banks or building societies goes bust.

You should also keep an eye on the inflation rate because a high rate can devalue the purchasing power of your savings. If you put £100 away and get 5% interest on it at a time when the inflation rate is also 5%, you won't be any better off (you'll end up with £105 in the bank, but that extra fiver will only buy you this year what £100 bought you last year). In fact, it's even worse than that because you will pay tax on your £5, which leaves standard-rate taxpayers with £4, meaning their money is actually worth less than it was a year ago. Conversely, periods of deflation increase the real worth of your savings because the value of your savings increases in relation to the cost of living.

CHECKLIST

- ✔ Forty per cent of Britons have no savings safety net.
- ✔ Savings help you cope with emergencies and give you a sense of security.
- ✔ Different kinds of savings account get different levels of interest – it's worth shopping around.
- ✔ The rate of inflation (or deflation) affects the real value of your savings.

2.
How to save

I **recently had a conversation** with a friend who had just moved house and found the passbook to an old savings account that she'd forgotten about. It had a balance of £100 and she hadn't touched it for 10 years. 'How much was in there?' I asked her, expecting that the compound interest over a decade would have been quite substantial. 'When I took it to my local branch they told me my balance was £102.' Two measly quid for 10 years' worth of saving? I couldn't believe it!

I worked out that my friend had been earning an average of 0.2% interest a year. If she had left that £100 in an account paying 5% interest annually, at the end of 10 years she would have had around £162. Clearly, making sure you put your savings into the right kind of account can make a big difference. And putting your money away for a decent period of time allows it to benefit from compound interest. What compound interest means is that instead of getting 5% interest paid on £100 in the second year, you get 5% on the original £100 plus the interest already received, in this case £5. Assuming the interest rate stays at 5%, in Year 2 it would pay £5.25, in Year 3 it would pay £5.51 and so on.

Regular amounts

Have a look at the budget you prepared earlier in the book and work out how much money you could save each month rather than spend. Whether it's a fiver, 20 quid or a couple of hundred, I recommend that you set up a regular transfer for that amount from your current account to your savings account. And then forget about it. Seriously. Try to see the amount you put into your savings each month the way you see the money that leaves your account to pay for your mobile phone or electricity bill. Forget you ever had it and get used to the fact that you put away a certain amount each month. Over time, you will find setting aside a fixed regular sum becomes easier because your finances will adjust to your savings commitment.

The longer you can leave your savings, the more you will accrue and the more options you will have. The great thing about regular savings is that they often attract the best interest rates. Banks can't afford to pay the highest rates on the biggest deposits, so they encourage saving by offering attractive rates to regular smaller amounts. These higher rates are sometimes only offered for the first year, so after twelve months, you simply look around for a high-interest account from a different bank. You'd be mad not to.

Lump sums

It's too easy to put money into a savings account and think you've done your bit. Like my friend who effectively threw away years of decent interest in her forgotten account, if you don't pay attention to your savings, the chances are they won't be working very hard for you. If you have a decent sum to put away, it pays to pay attention to the financial news.

Firstly, make sure that your money is in an account that's covered by the Financial Services Compensation Scheme that covers the first £50,000 of any deposit. Only money in banks with a UK banking licence is fully covered, so check with your bank that your money is safe.

The next thing you need to do is to separate your lump sum into an amount to put in an instant access account for emergencies, an amount to put in a notice account for money you might need; for example, if you lost your job, and an amount you can lock away for the long term.

Even in a period of low interest rates, there will still be some banks and building societies offering better-than-average deals to new customers, so the smart thing is to shop around to make use of bonus introductory rates. If you are prepared to move your money around regularly, it can make a big difference to the amount you earn. Just check the small print: sometimes the deals that look too good to be true come with some catches if, for example, you take your money out too early or let your balance drop below a certain amount.

Keep a close eye on the Best Buy tables in the weekend newspaper supplements for the new deals. And if you're not sure how much interest you're currently getting on your savings, call up your bank and ask.

Tax-efficient savings

All UK taxpayers have to pay tax on the interest they earn on savings. Your bank automatically deducts 20% from the interest they pay you, but if you're a higher-rate taxpayer, you'll have more tax to pay when you fill in your tax return. When interest rates are low, paying tax on the interest can make saving seem like a mug's game, which is why it's so important to make your savings work as tax efficiently as possible.

One way to do this is to put your money into overseas banks in territories that don't charge tax. However, you should be careful: thousands of savers opted for the tax-free choice of the Guernsey branch of Icesave; when its parent company went bust in September 2008, they discovered that they weren't covered by the FSCS insurance and lost their savings. Those who had their money in the UK arm of Icesave were able to recover their savings.

The other option for tax-efficient savings is to use up your ISA (Individual Savings Account) allowance. Each year, the government lets you save a certain amount tax-free. In 2008/09, the limit for cash savings was £3,600. With an ISA, the money in your account remains tax-free for life, so if you use up your ISA allowance each year you could slowly build up substantial savings that you will never have to pay tax on (unless of course, a future government changes the rules). Because of this tax advantage, it makes sense to keep your ISA account for long-term savings and not the funds you think you'll need to dip into occasionally or in the event of an emergency: once you have taken money out of your ISA account, you can't put money back in and still get the same tax exemption. You can also use your ISA allowance to invest in shares, which we will come to shortly.

 **CHECKLIST**

✔ Maximise the return you get on your savings by getting the highest possible interest rate.

✔ Even putting a little bit away each month eventually adds up to a significant sum.

✔ Make sure your deposits are covered by FSCS protection.

✔ You can save up to £3,600 each year tax-free in an ISA.

3.
Develop your own investment strategy

If savings are the safe way to provide for your future, investments are the riskier way. Despite the risks, I still think that once your savings have reached a comfortable level, you should start looking into your investment options. While your savings will never go down, your investments might. Investments are always sold on the basis of the rewards they offer, and the risks are always in the small print, so let me spell it out:

THE VALUE OF YOUR INVESTMENTS
CAN GO DOWN AS WELL AS UP.

However, where there's a risk, there's the chance of a reward. And if you get your investment strategy right, the rewards can be pretty big.

As I run through the different investment options, I want you to keep asking yourself that same old question: 'What are they getting out of it?' None of us likes being charged over the odds for financial services and advice, but I've reluctantly had to admit that unless people are incentivised to make money for themselves, they won't be incentivised to make money for you. Some of the people who run big investment funds charge a whopping 20% of profits, but because they stand to make such a spectacular pay packet, they are seriously motivated to make a spectacular return for their investors.

If you are not prepared, or capable, of managing your own investments, you'll be at the mercy of the professional investors you entrust with your cash. It is therefore essential to find the most able firms and individuals to look after your funds. Personally, I've worked too hard for my money to entrust it to anyone else to look after. I have always invested in myself and my businesses and the only companies I have owned shares in are companies I've had a say in running. The only time I have lost money in my career was when I bought £1 million worth of shares in a company I was planning to take over, but the company went bust before I could get control of it. This taught me that it's absolutely crucial to do your research when you make an investment. Thankfully, it wasn't all the money I had and it was an amount I could afford to lose. Thinking about how much you are prepared to risk is something you should be doing as you read on. Here are my rules of how to invest safely and profitably.

1. Take responsibility

Whether you put your money in stocks and shares or buy-to-let property, the best way to ensure the best possible return is to take responsibility for your money. Even if you have instructed a fund manager or financial adviser to invest it on your behalf, it's still important that you scrutinise the professionals' choices. If you chose an investment company because you rated a particular manager, you'll then want to know if that manager changes jobs and is no longer in charge of your funds. Being responsible means being engaged, which means keeping an eye on the financial news so you can discuss your investment options sensibly with your financial advisers. Being responsible means not blaming anyone else, or the market, the economic cycle or luck if you don't get the returns you are looking for. When I look around at the wealthiest people I know, the single characteristic they share is their willingness to be responsible for their financial decisions.

2. Spread the return

I've talked quite a lot about economic cycles, so one of the important questions you need to ask yourself is when you want a return on your investment. Let's say you are investing for your retirement in 20 years' time, but in 20 years' time there is a recession and the stock and property markets are depressed. Just at the time you want to get your hands on your money, it's worth less than you had planned for. There's very little any of us can do about the economic cycle, but we can make contingencies.

In this scenario you might have the option of retiring later, but the best way of dealing with the worst the economic cycle has to offer is to spread the window you want a return in. Planning so that your investments don't all mature at the same time means that you can insulate yourself from the worst the markets have to throw at you.

Spreading your investments into short-, medium- and long-term bets is the best way to do this. Look for safer investments for the long term, less risky ones for the medium, but in the short term you could put a smaller amount into some chancier options. If you are willing to manage your short-term investments and buy and sell them at the most opportune moments, you create the chance to make a lot of money.

3. Spread your investments

The golden rule of investment is to spread your risk by not putting all your money into one venture (although if you are investing in your own business this will be a rule you will probably have to break). If you went to a stockbroker for advice, he would probably tell you to put your money in a range of stocks in a range of markets. If you went to a property expert, you'd be told not to use all your cash to buy one property, but to split your deposit and buy two properties with the help of mortgages. By and large, professional advisers have to be cautious: if they take risks with their clients' money that don't pay off, they'll be out of business. If, however, they make a modest return, they get another year to get it right.

Broadly speaking, this is good advice, but I don't see the point in spreading your investments so thinly that you don't give yourself the chance to make a return when the opportunity is there. If you buy a pound's worth of shares in a thousand companies, you haven't invested – or risked, if you prefer – enough to get a recent return, or reward. My strategy is to split funds between different kinds of investments. The most important of these is the home in which you live. Buying a decent property that you can live happily in and afford comfortably is the foundation of my investment strategy. Not only will you be slowly paying off your mortgage, but if the property increases in value – which history tells us it will, if only eventually – any gains are tax-free.

I would then put some of your remaining money in the stock market (I'll go into more detail on this shortly) in a mix of companies, funds and territories. Some of your shares should be invested for long-term growth, and some for short-term income. Making an additional investment in buy-to-let property has the benefit of providing both a likely capital gain in the long term with a fairly stable income. In both cases, timing your entry into the market is vital. Unlike buying a home, you can time buying investments to coincide with an upturn in the market. Entering a market in decline makes no sense at all. The key to smart investing is not to rush when you don't have to.

4. Spread the risk

Finally, a good all-round investment strategy involves putting some of your money in safe bets, but occasionally risking a small proportion of your wealth on the kinds of investments that provide the chance for significant returns. The risk:reward ratio means you're more likely to lose your money if the risk is great, but then so too are the rewards if things go your way. In practice, this might mean buying shares in exciting – and risky – start-up ventures via the Alternative Investment Market (AIM) as well as some boring, but safer, shares in blue chip companies on the main stock exchange. Or putting some money into property – a traditional safe bet – and some into gilts and bonds, and some into shares. Knowing you're likely to get a return on your safer investments means you can swallow the losses if your riskier bets fail to pay off.

CHECK LIST

- ✔ Investments can go down as well as up.
- ✔ The riskier investments sometimes offer the best rewards.
- ✔ You can minimise your risk by developing a sound investment strategy.
- ✔ Having a range of types of investments and a wide window for taking the returns gives you the greatest flexibility.

4.
Own your own home
(if you possibly can)

Even though the prices of property can go down as well as up – and even though at the time of writing I am aware that thousands of homeowners are struggling with the painful reality of 'negative equity' – I still think owning your own home is one of the smartest financial decisions you can make. And that's not just because history tells us that the property market always bounces back.

Let me demonstrate. Let's assume that you buy a property for £100,000 in a world where the property market remains static. If you take out a 25-year mortgage to pay for that property, at the end of the loan you would own the property outright. If you rented the same house, you would be paying rent for ever. I remember when I bought my first house, one of my friends asked me if I was worried about getting into so much debt (which seems laughable now as I bought that house for £12,000!). I could see why she was concerned because we had saved so hard to get our deposit together that we hadn't any money for furniture! Even though we were living in one room while we saved up to furnish the rest of the house, I still thought the way we were living made more sense than renting. I told my friend that she was actually in more debt than me as she would still owe rent long after I had paid my mortgage off. The way I saw it, her rent would be a debt she would pay for the rest of her life.

Even without house prices rising, I believe you are better off buying than renting, especially as mortgage payments are usually lower than rents. However, over the long term, house prices have historically always risen, which gives homeowners a fantastic opportunity to amass some wealth. And under current legislation, any rises are tax-free.

Unlike many other kinds of investments, you have a lot of control over your home. While you can't dictate who your neighbours are, you can choose to buy a home in an area that is likely to remain or become desirable – a major influence over how much your home will increase in value by. You can also decorate your home in a way that will help it hold or increase its value, and carry out home improvements that will add more to the value of your home than they cost to implement. Not only that, but you also get to live in it and make a home for your family!

Mortgages

Most property in the UK is bought with a mortgage and there are two very good reasons for this. Firstly, very few people can afford to buy a property without one, but even for those who can, it actually makes financial sense to get a mortgage. Let me explain: let's say you have a £50,000 deposit and you buy a £200,000 property with a £150,000 mortgage. If, when you come to sell, your property is worth £300,000, you get to keep all the profit and the bank just gets its mortgage repaid. Because banks don't take equity stakes in your property, you can use a mortgage to leverage the return you get on your £50,000. By marrying your money with the bank's money, you get the growth on a £200,000 investment rather than a £50,000 one.

Not only have all housing markets risen over time, but inflation has consistently eaten away at the real value of any money you have. While this is pretty soul-destroying for savers, inflation is a boon for borrowers as over time the amount you owe is reduced in real terms. If you take out a £150,000 mortgage this year, in 10 years' time your £150,000 debt will feel a lot smaller as inflation will have reduced the value of £150k (deflation, of course, has the opposite effect and increases the real value of your debt). Even if your property hasn't increased greatly in value, the impact of inflation will mean that your repayments tend to become more manageable over time, whereas rents increase with inflation.

So now I hope I've persuaded you that home ownership makes financial sense even in a flat property market, I want to look at mortgages in more detail. At any one time there will be thousands of different mortgage products on the market and it can be virtually impossible to work out which is the best mortgage for you. Essentially, there are two types of mortgage – repayment and interest only. Obviously, a repayment mortgage pays back the original loan (plus interest, of course) whereas an interest-only mortgage only repays the interest; at the end of the mortgage term you will still owe the original loan amount, or 'principal'. Because you are not repaying the principal, monthly payments on interest-only mortgages are lower. However, you need to have a plan as to how you will repay the principal – perhaps with savings, investments or downsizing to a smaller property – otherwise you will be in the position of always having to pay a mortgage like a tenant paying rent.

Choosing a repayment or an interest-only mortgage is possibly the easy bit. You must also select from the following options:

Fixed rate

Fixed-rate mortgages guarantee a particular interest rate for a fixed period of time. If you are concerned about rising interest rates, then fixing can offer peace of mind. However, they sometimes come with arrangement fees and redemption penalties if you sell your home before the end of the fixed term. And if interest rates fall, you will be left paying the higher rate. At the end of the fixed-rate period, you may be obliged to stay on your lender's standard variable rate (sometimes advertised just as the 'SVR') for a time or pay a penalty. Lenders' variable rates rarely offer good value.

Tracker mortgages

These loans guarantee to follow the base rate, sometimes for the entire duration of the mortgage. They are usually a per cent or two above the base rate (although some introductory rates are below the base rate), so if interest rates come down, your mortgage payments will decrease, but if they go up, so will your monthly outgoings.

Variable rate

If you are only going to have a mortgage for a short period, it can sometimes be worth going on to a lender's variable rate as these tend not to have arrangement fees or redemption penalties. Once you factor in the entry and exit costs of some mortgages, it can work out cheaper to pay a higher monthly premium for the life of the loan.

Cap and Collar

The rates on these mortgages have a ceiling and a floor. So if the Bank of England rate goes up to 10% but you have agreed a cap of 7% that's how much your bank will charge you. However, if the BoE rate falls to 2% but you have agreed a collar of 5%, you will pay the higher rate. I think these deals give you some of the upside of falling rates while protecting you from the downside of rising rates.

Offset mortgages

If you have savings, some loans allow you to offset the amount you have saved against the amount you have borrowed. Let's say you have a mortgage of £100,000 and savings of £10,000, with an offset mortgage you would only pay interest on £90,000, which usually works out cheaper than paying interest on £100,000 and receiving a lower rate of interest on your £10,000 savings.

There are countless variations on these mortgages, so it is important to shop around for the best deal. Best Buy tables in the newspapers can be helpful, but you will almost certainly need a mortgage broker to find the right deal for you. Don't forget to ask how a broker gets paid though: some are paid a commission for selling certain financial products, so make sure you know if they are incentivised to offer one deal over another. You can then make a judgement as to whether you're getting the best advice or not.

Deposits

There is one really big catch with mortgages – you need a deposit. Although there was a time around the new millennium when lenders were offering 100% loans – even 125% loans in some circumstances – banks usually only give mortgages to people who have saved up a deposit. As I've already said, banks don't like taking risks, so by asking you to come up with a deposit they minimise their exposure to risk on two fronts. Firstly, if you have a deposit you are likely to be financially responsible, but secondly, and crucially, your deposit insulates the bank from any potential decrease in the value of the property you are buying. If you buy a house for £200,000 with a £20,000 deposit and a £180,000 mortgage that you then sell at a loss for £180,000 because the housing market has slumped by 10%, the bank will get all its money back but you won't get any of yours. Just as the banks don't ask for a stake in any growth, nor do they take a stake in any losses.

The bigger the deposit you have, the more you insulate the bank from any risk. When the risks are reduced, they are prepared to take a smaller reward, which is why the best interest rates are reserved for customers with the biggest deposits.

In a buoyant housing market, 90% and 95% mortgages are

common, but when the housing market slumps, banks start asking for bigger deposits before they are happy to lend. The worse the housing market gets, the fewer risks banks will take and they change the sorts of mortgages they offer, as well as the fees required to get a mortgage.

The size of the mortgage you will be offered doesn't just relate to the size of your deposit, but to the size of your income. Traditionally, banks have lent between three and four times an applicant's salary. So if you earn £20,000 a year, you can expect a bank to be prepared to lend you between £60,000 and £80,000.

Additional costs

When you buy a property, there are additional costs that it's easy to overlook. Solicitors, stamp duty, removals, repairs, agent's fees, broker's charges – the bills can really add up. Knowing in advance what your likely costs will be will help you budget for them:

1. Stamp duty

This is a tax payable on all property purchases costing more than £125,000 (raised temporarily to £175,000 in December 2008 to boost the property market). For properties costing between £125,000 and £250,000, the stamp duty is 1% of the sale price (i.e. if you buy a property for £240,000 your stamp duty bill will be £2,400), 3% for properties worth between £250,000 and £500,000, and 4% on properties worth more than £500,000.

2. Conveyancing

This is the term to describe the legal work involved in buying a property. It doesn't have to be done by a solicitor but it's advisable that it is. Solicitors usually have a sliding scale of fees depending on how much the property costs, whether it is leasehold or freehold, whether you're buying and selling simultaneously and whether the sale is part of a chain. Costs can vary wildly – and so can the service. Personally, I would be happy to pay extra for a solicitor who answers their own phone and is on the ball. Budget for a fee of £400 to £1,000, but get quotes from three firms before you instruct a conveyancer.

3. Removals

If you're buying your first home you might be able to move yourself with the help of a few friends and the cost will be no more than van hire and pizzas. If you have a lot of possessions, moving yourself can be very difficult and stressful at a time when there is so much else to organise. The cost varies depending on the distance to your new property, ease of access and the amount of possessions. Get quotes from several removal companies but expect a charge of £500 to £1,000 for a two- or three-bed property.

4. Arrangement fees

Some mortgage products have additional upfront fees on top of the monthly repayments. In most cases you can add these to your debt, but you may choose to pay them up front. In some cases, the broker who arranged your financing might also require a fee.

5. Agent's fees

If you are selling an existing property, the chances are that you will be selling it through an estate agent, which means you will have to deduct their fee from the sale price. Estate agents usually charge between 1% and 2% (plus VAT) of the sale price. On a £200,000 property, an agent charging 1.5% will hand you an invoice for £3450.25 assuming a VAT rate of 1.5%.

6. Repairs and renovations

Even if you are buying a brand-new property, it's likely that you'll have some DIY to do. In older properties, the cost of new kitchens, bathrooms, curtains and carpets quickly add up. In the case of major renovations, you should get quotes from a couple of builders before you make an offer for the property so that you have a realistic idea of how much it will actually cost you to make it liveable.

7. Furnishings

As I've already said, when I bought my first home, we couldn't afford furniture and lived in one room until we had saved up enough to buy furniture and appliances for the rest of the house. If you're not prepared to live like this, you need to budget in advance for the things you'll need.

The good news is that if you are buying a property as an investment, most of these expenses can be deducted from the amount you might eventually have to pay in capital gains tax. If you're buying property to live in, the good news is at least now you know what to expect!

Affordability

So far, I've talked about the benefits of home ownership, but there is a downside. If you buy a property at the height of a booming market and the market then slumps, you can find yourself paying a mortgage that is worth more than the property, a situation called 'negative equity'. At the time of writing, property prices had fallen by 16% in the preceding year (and of course that figure doesn't include the properties that *couldn't* sell in a depressed market), leaving thousands of people in negative equity. While this is pretty galling, it's not necessarily catastrophic if you can still afford your monthly mortgage payments and you enjoy living in the property.

However, if your income drops or your mortgage payments go up and you can't afford to make your payments, you can get into trouble. If you fall behind with your repayments, your lender may start proceedings to repossess the property. There is some protection from repossession in the form of government help (if your mortgage is less than £400,000) so as soon as you think you might be in trouble, you should talk to your lender and get some advice from an organisation such as Citizens Advice Bureaux. If your property is repossessed, it's likely your lender will try to sell it – possibly at auction – to get their money back. They won't care if there's anything left over for you, and if the sale price was less than the mortgage, you will *still* be liable for repaying the difference.

During the last housing crash, there were stories of people simply putting their house keys through the letterbox of their bank and walking away from their debt, and I thought that was the worst thing they could do. Once the bank repossessed their property and (in all likelihood) sold it at a loss at auction, the former homeowner would still owe the bank the difference between the sale price and the mortgage – yet they wouldn't have an asset that would in time increase in value to repay that debt.

You always have to weigh up the costs of renting with the cost of paying a mortgage. Month by month you are probably no better off if you rent, and in the long run you are almost certainly worse off *and* your credit rating will be shot. Painful as negative equity is, holding on to the property – either by taking in a lodger or renting it out while you move somewhere cheaper – is almost certainly the cheapest and least painful way of eventually repaying that debt.

Of course, if you've bought a property you don't enjoy living in, the temptation to walk away is all the greater, so no matter how good an investment property might seem, it's always a better investment if it's also a happy home. If you wouldn't be happy living in it in tough times, don't buy it. When you're looking at a property to buy, ask yourself the following:

- **Is it big enough for your family?**
- **Is it in a good neighbourhood?**
- **Are there any nearby developments that might affect its value (either positively or negatively)?**
- **Is it in a good state of repair?**

The best way to make sure you don't get into trouble with your mortgage payments is to work out whether you can really afford the property in the first place. When you take out your mortgage and are told what your monthly payments will be, stop and decide if you have enough coming in to cover the mortgage as well as all your other commitments. Just because a bank is willing to lend to you doesn't mean you can afford the loan.

In business, when I start a new venture or take on new financing, I carry out a sensitivity analysis, and I think you should do it for your private finances too. A sensitivity analysis involves working out how much your income can drop by, or how much your expenses can go up by, before you go into the red. Work out how much your repayments would be if interest rates went up by 2%, 5% or 7%. Then calculate the minimum you would need to earn and still be able to keep up with your repayments. Your age will probably play a significant role in the comfort level you are happy with. In your twenties, you might feel a 20% margin for movement – a 10% rise in prices and a 10% drop in earnings – is comfortable, but in your fifties, you might have enough to weather bigger financial storms and be comfortable with a 40% or 50% shift in fortunes.

CHECKLIST

✔ Owning your own home has many advantages over renting.

✔ The type of mortgage you get can have a big impact on your monthly payments.

✔ Even if things get tight financially and your property value dips into negative equity, it still pays to keep up with your mortgage payments.

✔ Conducting a sensitivity analysis will let you see how secure your finances are.

5.
Property as an investment

Property is seen by many people, including me, as a good long-term investment. The fact is that people will always need somewhere to live, and there are certain demographic trends that mean the UK property market is likely to recover from any house price slump. Firstly, our population is growing more quickly than we can build houses; secondly more people are delaying marriage till later in life; and thirdly we have a pretty high divorce rate. These three things mean that there is going to be more continuing demand for homes. The laws of supply and demand mean property is likely to produce good long-term returns.

Gains made on your home, although potentially significant, tend not to make a marked difference to your life for the very simple reason that if your home has appreciated in value, so will other properties. Your home may have increased in value from £200,000 to £300,000, but that £100,000 gain can only be spent if you downsize to a smaller property or leave the property market altogether. If you had made a £100,000 gain on an investment property, however, you could sell it and release the cash to spend on whatever you wanted (although you do pay capital gains tax on any gains, and any income is subject to income tax). If you can invest in property at the beginning of an upward curve in house prices, it's actually pretty hard to lose money, despite the fees and upfront costs, but that doesn't mean there aren't pitfalls.

Buy-to-let

When house prices rose in the 1990s, hundreds of thousands of Britons remortgaged their own homes to release some of the equity they had built up. In exchange for slightly higher mortgage payments, they had deposits to buy second properties with. The mortgage payments on these properties were covered by renting them out. Buy-to-let investors stood to get capital growth on two properties instead of one, and when both mortgages were paid off, the income from one would provide a pension that would let them live in the other, *even if property prices didn't increase*. No wonder so many people became landlords. Of course, plenty of people didn't stop at two properties, and as soon as there was enough equity accrued in their 'property portfolio', they remortgaged to release more equity and bought another investment property.

The boom in buy-to-let led to bust when the oversupply of rented properties saw rental income slump, which meant some landlords were out of pocket each month. For those with several properties, this led to bankruptcy and repossession. As the housing market started to decline in 2007, many landlords were facing negative equity. Those who had bought properties with interest-only mortgages saw their debt stretching out into the future with no hope of ever being repaid. Landlords can lose – and make – money in two ways: they are reliant on both the rental market to firstly make a profit each month, and then the property market to provide capital gains in the long term. Performing a sensitivity analysis would have insulated amateur landlords from the worst of the house price slump.

Banks offer specialist buy-to-let mortgages where the amount they are prepared to lend isn't just determined by the purchase price of the property and the buyer's income, but also on the rental value of the property. Because buy-to-let is seen as riskier than owner-occupation, banks compensate for this risk by charging higher rates on commercial mortgages and they may ask for certain covenants, perhaps that the rent will never fall below a certain level, or that the mortgage won't ever be greater than 80% of the value of the property. So if rents were to fall or house prices to drop, in theory you would break your covenant with the bank and the loan could be recalled.

The upside

For me, property is a good investment as you can retain a lot of control. You can choose where and what you buy, you can decide who you rent it out to, when to remortgage and when to sell. It can also provide you with a monthly income as well as the potential for capital growth. And as long as you have bought it with a repayment mortgage, your tenants are effectively repaying your debt for you. If you can manage the investment successfully for the lifetime of the mortgage, once it's paid off you get an income in perpetuity.

All the expenses you incur as a landlord are tax-deductible, even the interest on your mortgage. However, the expenses are pretty high – from stamp duty (4% on properties worth more than £500,000), the agent's fees and legal costs. Currently, you pay 18% CGT, a lower rate of tax than even the basic 20% paid on income tax, on any gains above £9,600. If you are a higher-rate taxpayer, making money through investments rather than income is very tax-efficient. Should the property become your main home for any period of time, you can also avoid paying capital gains tax on some of the profit.

The downside

For a lot of people, managing a property is too much hassle and so they choose to invest in the stock market instead. If you're not prepared to deal with a fair amount of hassle, property investment probably isn't for you. The biggest headache is finding and dealing with tenants. Although letting agents can find you tenants, they charge as much as 8% of the annual rent, plus another 5% or so to manage the property. Needless to say, in terms of financial return, the smart way to find tenants is without professional help, either through advertising or word-of-mouth, and then manage the property yourself.

Once you have found tenants, you really should vet them by taking out references from their employer, previous landlord and bank. Without references, you may find it expensive to get insurance, even if you are letting the property unfurnished. You are now legally obliged to lodge your tenant's deposit with the Deposit Protection Service (www.depositprotection.com) as well as getting gas and electrical safety certificates.

If you're lucky, you'll get tenants who'll take good care of the property, always pay their rent and hang around for years. If you're unlucky, you'll get tenants who don't pay the rent and trash your property, causing thousands of pounds' worth of damage. Which means the property will be unlettable until you've redecorated, which means you will almost certainly have 'void months' when no rent is coming in but the mortgage is still going out. And then there are service charges and maintenance costs that can really hurt if you are only just about breaking even.

Another downside of property investment is that it isn't a flexible investment. Properties can take months to sell even in buoyant markets, so if you want to cash in your investment you have to be patient. Although it's possible to remortgage properties fairly quickly to release equity, property isn't a liquid asset. And because you can't control the market, the best you can hope for is that you time things well enough to buy near the bottom of the market and sell near the top. I wouldn't worry too much about buying at the absolute bottom and selling at the absolute top: just buying and selling at broadly the right time is good enough, even for professional investors.

With so many potential pitfalls, carrying out a sensitivity analysis before becoming a landlord is absolutely vital. You should know how much rents can fall by, or your mortgage can increase by, before you're into the red each month. You also

need to know how many void months you can handle each
year, or how big a maintenance bill you can cope with before
it starts to hurt. I think a good level of comfort comes with
a 40% margin for change – either your income dropping by
40% or your income dropping by 20% while your costs rise
by the same proportion. Unless you are happy to supplement
your property investment in the short term in the hope of
long-term capital gains, a 40% cushion is what you should be
looking for.

CHECKLIST

✔ Investing in a second property creates the opportunity
  for capital gains as well as regular income.

✔ Expenses are deductible against tax.

✔ Dealing with tenants can be a real headache.

✔ Property isn't a flexible investment.

6.
How to invest in stocks and shares

As I've already said, the only stocks and shares I've ever held have been in my own companies. I would rather invest in my own business than someone else's, but as most people don't start their own businesses, investing in other people's is quite tempting. Although fortunes have been slashed by the recent market turbulence, most professionals believe that the stock market will always rise in the end. Before I move on to what I think is a sensible approach to investing in stocks and shares, I want to share my concerns.

Why you *shouldn't* invest in shares

Buying shares is a complicated business – deciding what sector to buy in, which companies to snap up, which ones to sell etc – which is why most investors rely on middle-men to make their investment decisions for them. As someone who believes passionately that we prosper when we take responsibility for our financial decisions, this is something I'm pretty sceptical about. No broker is ever going to care as much as you do about your money, no matter what level of commission they stand to earn. If a broker invests your money badly, they just won't get a bonus whereas you have lost your life savings. There's an imbalance there that will always make me uncomfortable, but that doesn't mean that all brokers are useless – some can make you very rich.

Markets do collapse periodically, whether it's the stock market as a whole or just a particular sector, and if your shares are

in the wrong companies, you can make very big losses. While
market statistics show an upward curve over time, these gen-
eralised figures mask spectacular falls in individual stocks that
have left some investors broke. However, if you're smart and
you pay attention, you should be able to minimise your losses
– or even avoid them.

In 2008, a Barclays Capital Equity-Gilt study assessed
stock-market performance over the past 50 years and discovered that – when adjusted for inflation – the stock market had
produced an average return of 7.2% a year. Compared to putting money into savings accounts – which the same study concluded produced returns of 1% when figures were adjusted for
inflation – I guess this is a pretty good return. What this means
is if you invested £1,000, at the end of 10 years of average
growth, your shares would be worth £2,004; it's not bad, but
frankly it's not enough to get me very excited. Nor, I suspect,
most people who buy stocks and shares in the misguided hope
that they will buy a share for £1 that they will sell for £100.
It's also worth pointing out that the past 50 years have, by and
large, been boom years. If the survey had covered 100 years
and included the Depression of the 1930s, I suspect the figure
would be significantly lower.

Although markets always rise in the end, individual shares
don't necessarily. Take the FTSE 100 index, the list of the 100
biggest companies listed on the London Stock Exchange. The
index rises over time because it is a best-seller chart – the
poorly performing companies drop out of the chart and are
replaced by strong performers. It is perfectly possible to own
shares in companies that go down the pan while the market as
a whole motors ahead.

Determining which companies are likely to do well involves
a lot of research and that's something most of us don't have
time for. Not even brokers have the time to research every
company on the stock exchange (there are more than 900 on
the London exchange alone and thousands more worldwide),
which is why so many brokers adopt a herd mentality. When
they see a rival buy – or sell – a share, they think their rival

must know something they don't and follow suit, and that's why we get surges and collapses in share prices.

I suppose my biggest problem with the stock market is that most of the people who get rich from share trading are the traders. They can get million-pound bonuses for getting their clients 7.2% returns, and I'm just not very comfortable with that. Brokers often charge a fee for the actual buying or selling of a share – which means they make money whether or not it's a wise trade – and frequently charge an annual management fee of around 1% of the total money you invest with them, which again means they make their money whether or not they have performed well.

For all this though, I can't deny that in 2008 – before the worst of the stock-market falls – the richest man in the world was not an entrepreneur or an inventor, he was a share trader. And despite the stock-market crash, Warren Buffett, an American billionaire, is still worth 10 or 20 times what I'm worth, so it's no wonder that so many people put their faith in the stock markets.

I have one last niggle about investing in shares and it's this: the price you are quoted is never the price you pay. Just like when you buy foreign currency before a holiday, shares are bought for one price, but sold for a lower price. This is called the 'bid/ask spread' and is effectively a commission levied on each trade, on top of the actual commission. If I bought a £1 stock, I'd probably have to pay £1.02 for it, but if I sold it, I'd only get 98p. Generally, the less trade there has been on a stock, the bigger the spread. If you scale up those figures for big transactions, that's quite a lot of money that simply disappears.

And why you *should* invest in stocks and shares

When a company is floated on the stock exchange, it raises millions of pounds from investors that it uses to grow the business that produce returns, which in turn raise the value of the shares. By investing in shares, you allow the economy to grow and entrepreneurs like me to create wealth. You gain, but we all gain through your investment. Potentially, the gains for you are enormous; people do occasionally buy a small quantity of stock that experiences spectacular growth and makes them a phenomenal amount of cash. And even if you don't manage spectacular growth, that 7.2% growth means you double your money every 10 years, which isn't terrible.

Like property, share-based investment gives you two shots at an income: the first from capital growth and the second from dividend payments. Dividends are a proportion of the annual profits paid to shareholders when the company's board decides it is prudent to do so.

As long as you are young enough to see through a couple of economic downturns and you are prepared to look over your broker's shoulder occasionally – or trade yourself – you have a chance of making some money. The closer you are to retirement, the riskier stocks and shares become, even if you are holding them for dividend payments rather than capital growth. If you retire expecting an income from your shares just as the market nosedives, you may find you have a lot less money to live off than you had planned. The older you are, the less time you have to make up for any losses, so moving your investment into less volatile gilts and bonds is usually advised. Stock-market investment, though I hate to say it, is a young man's game.

Of course, you don't have to invest in individual companies – a huge proportion of money invested in the stock market is done through funds. You buy shares in a fund that is managed by a broker who buys and sells individual shares on behalf of the fund. By taking a stake in so many companies, this min- imises the risk, but also the potential rewards. There are thou- sands of different funds operated by hundreds of different brokerages. Some specialise in specific sectors – pharmaceuti- cal, technology, commodities etc – some in specific locations (South America, China, Europe etc). You don't have to put all your money into one fund. In one year you might choose to put some cash into a green fund, another year into a fund specialising in telecoms. This strategy spreads the risk and insulates you if one sector, or one economy, collapses.

Generally, the more volatile the markets are, the more opportunities there are to make big gains and big losses. In 2008, the property developer Barratt's share price dropped a whopping 96% from its peak – one of the most spectacular share price falls I've ever heard of. While this was terrible for anyone who held Barratt shares prior to the collapse, it was an opportunity for others to pick them up for a bargain and wait until the housing forecast, and Barratt's figures, improved. The same could be said for the banking sector. The recent turmoil has left banking stocks at a fraction of their previous values; while there might be more volatility to come, those looking for long-term gains might see an opportunity.

Using a broker

The best way to find a broker is through a recommendation, and if that's not an option you can find one through research. Reading the financial press will give you suggestions for able operators that you can then check out online. Once you've found a broker you would like to manage your money for you, there are some questions you need to ask him or her:

What kind of broker are they?

Some will only buy and sell shares when you tell them to. Some will give you advice and then complete the trades for you. Others will simply buy and sell as they see fit.

What are their fees?

Find out how the brokers are remunerated and how much their services will cost you. Find out if there are any penalties when you sell your shares and if they will deduct tax at source.

How often can you talk to them?

Do they have a freephone number you can call whenever you want a review? Will they produce an annual report for you? Or will you never hear from them again?

What happens if they leave the company?

If you have chosen an individual broker, who would manage your funds if they left?

You want to be sure that your broker understands what your ambitions for your investment are. Do you want a monthly income from dividend payments or long-term growth? Do you want to invest ethically and avoid companies that profit from things like tobacco and oil? It shouldn't just be you interviewing your potential broker: if your broker doesn't ask you very many questions, I would be doubtful that they could produce returns for you.

Trading yourself

Of course, you don't need a broker. The internet has made it easy to do the trading yourself – the difficult bit is deciding which shares to buy. Two seconds on Google will give you several self-trade sites where you can buy shares for a flat fee (usually between £10 and £15, but this fee usually reduces if you do a lot of trading) plus the 0.5% stamp duty payable on all share purchases. Some also charge an annual handling charge – perhaps half a per cent of your total holding.

Some people are tempted to 'day trade', which basically means doing the work of a broker from home, and they buy and sell throughout the day depending on market movements. I would never recommend that you do this – day trading is a specialist's game that can be time-consuming to do well and expensive if done badly. Instead, I think you could learn a thing of two from Warren Buffett, who has made his fortune by buying significant stakes in major corporations – McDonald's, Coca-Cola, Gillette – and holding on to those stocks for a very long time.

If you work in a particular industry and have good sector knowledge about smart chief executives and can spot trends that will affect a company's performance, you may be better placed than many brokers to invest in your industry. Selecting a handful of companies to invest in that you have knowledge of and that you believe are well placed to prosper seems like a very sensible strategy to me.

The conventional view is that the bigger stake you take, the less of an impact the transaction charges eat into your shares (whether you buy £1,000 or £100 of shares, you will still pay the flat rate of, say, £12 to trade). Equally, the less you trade, the less those trading fees eat into your profit. If you are new to trading, I would not recommend that you jump into the market with your nest egg and buy thousands of pounds' worth of shares. Why don't you select a couple of stocks initially and buy a few hundred pounds' worth. Write off the transaction charges – see them as a learning fee – and see what happens to your shares. You might be disappointed with the growth or surprised at how volatile they are, or you might just kick yourself that you didn't buy more shares. Starting small gives you a taste of what you might experience if you start to commit more money to the markets and how you might feel if you were to start to rely on shares to provide for your future.

If after an initial period you think that share dealing is for you, do your research into target companies you trust and understand. Read their annual reports, judge how robust you think they are and how plausible their growth projections are, and if you're still convinced they have room to grow, acquire some of their stock. Never buy more than you can afford to lose in any one company, but once you've bought them, learn from Mr Buffett and hold on to them for the long term. Don't be alarmed by market fluctuations – let the professionals trade their way through tumultuous times – and put your faith in the long-term gains the markets have traditionally offered.

Tax-efficient

Capital gains tax (CGT) is payable on profits from shares, although you can make up to £9,600 a year before you pay 18% CGT tax on the remainder of your gains. However, you can buy up to £7,200 worth of shares as part of your ISA allowance. All shares bought within an ISA are exempt from CGT and income tax, so whether your shares pay an income from dividends or increase in value, the gain is completely tax-free. However much you invest in the stock market, it makes sense to buy your first £7,200 worth of shares within an ISA. You can do this yourself via self-trade sites, or your broker can do this for you.

 **CHECKLIST**

- ✔ Individual shares can decline in value, even when the market as a whole rises. And vice versa of course.
- ✔ The average gain – adjusted for inflation – over the past 50 years has been 7.2% per annum.
- ✔ Holding stocks for a long time reduces exposure to short-term falls in share prices.
- ✔ Holding a variety of stocks in a variety of markets reduces risk.
- ✔ You don't have to use a broker – you can trade yourself online.
- ✔ You can put the first £7,200 of shares bought in any year into an ISA which means you won't pay tax on any income or gains.

7.
Your pension – something to look forward to?

On average, **our working lives** start when we're about 20 and end when we're in our sixties. When you think that the average life expectancy in Britain is now over 80, we need to earn enough in 40 years of work to keep us for 60 years of life. If you don't think about how you will keep yourself in retirement, you'll be at the mercy of whatever the state can afford to provide when you reach retirement age. Currently the basic state pension is £90.70 a week, which might – depending on your circumstances – be topped up with the second state pension (around another £40) and pension credits (which provide a minimum income guarantee of £124 a week for single people and £189 for a couple). There are also entitlements to housing benefit and council tax benefit that some pensioners can claim. It's just about enough to live on, but in the future, there's no guarantee that the state will be able to be so generous.

Some economists believe that Britain's ageing population means there is a pensions timebomb sitting under the economy that will blow up at some point. Meeting the needs of an increased number of pensioners while the size of the workforce decreases (which leads to less revenue being collected in taxes) means that future governments may not be able to provide anything like a liveable income. So if you're young enough to do something about it, I urge you to think seriously about how you will pay for your old age.

You might like the idea of carrying on working, but while many workers are willing, employers are less enthusiastic about an ageing workforce, despite age discrimination legislation, because older workers tend to take more time off sick, have reduced productivity rates and they're less likely to have up-to-date skills. Not every profession values experience, so you can't expect that you will be able to carry on working, even though I heard recently that Britons now consider themselves middle-aged until they hit 70.

There are still a few workers who stand to benefit from final salary pension schemes operated by corporations to encourage and reward long service. These pay out a percentage of a worker's final salary (typically 66%) as a pension for life. As these have become too expensive to maintain, it tends only to be people employed by the state – civil servants, police, fire brigade, health service professionals – who can expect anything like a final salary scheme, but even in these professions, new recruits are rarely allowed to join the pension club and instead must rely on a pension they provide for themselves.

The standard way to do this is via a personal pension, but I don't think these are right for many people. I don't think you necessarily need to get a pension (though there are two circumstances in which it's probably wise to), but you certainly need to get a plan.

Traditional pensions

Most pensions work like this: you put a proportion of your earnings into a fund that is invested by one of the big pension providers in the stock market, which hopefully increases substantially in value. Your pension provider earns their money by taking a percentage of your total fund as their annual fee (usually between 0.5% and 2%) whether or not your fund has performed well. Most pension fund managers are pretty cautious as they are obviously responsible for their clients' future income levels, and as that means they can be risk-averse, they often miss out on the best gains in the market. However, when you are investing in a pension, you are looking for security not spectacular growth, so the 7.2% average return that the market offers is probably enough.

When you retire, you are allowed to take 25% of your pension fund as a tax-free lump sum and you must buy an 'annuity' with the rest. An annuity is an insurance product that guarantees you an income for life and this income will be dependent on your health, family medical history and the age at which you retire. If you've got bad genes and the insurance company doesn't expect you to live until your nineties, you'll get a higher annuity than if you're likely to get a telegram from the king on your hundredth birthday. Your annuity is treated like any other source of income which means you will pay tax on it.

To encourage you to contribute to your pension fund, the government gives tax incentives. If you pay the basic rate of tax, currently 20%, the government will top up your contributions by that amount. So for every £80 you put in, the government puts in £20. If you are a higher-rate taxpayer, the contributions are more generous: for every £60 you put in, the government will put in £20 but you can also claim relief on your contribution worth another £20 when you complete your tax return each year. Given that you will pay at least 20% on any income from your pension, the benefit to basic-rate taxpayers is negligible, but for higher-rate taxpayers it's a bit of a gift. Being a higher-rate taxpayer is one of only two circumstances in which I would encourage you to take out a pension.

In exchange for these tax benefits, the government puts restrictions on your pension fund. Unlike other savings accounts, you cannot get access to your fund until you are 55 and you have no choice but to buy an annuity with 75% of your fund – even if you think the annuities you are offered represent bad value. For me, it's only the 40% contribution made by the government that makes up for those restrictions and the tax deducted from the eventual payments.

The other circumstance in which I think taking out a personal pension is a good idea is if your employer makes contributions. Some employers will match your own contributions (usually up to a ceiling of 5%), which means you'd be mad not to join their scheme if you can afford your own share of the contributions. However, make sure that your pension pot is portable and that you can take it with you when you change jobs.

For more advice on pensions, talk to the Pensions Advisory Service on 0845 601 2923.

Self-Invested Personal Pensions (SIPPs)

SIPPs are relatively new pension products that give those who want it a more active role in how their pension funds are invested. SIPPs still have the same tax advantages as personal pensions but they also allow holders to invest in a greater range of assets, like gilts and unit trusts, as well as commercial property. If you run a small business, it makes sense to buy your premises as part of your SIPP. Your SIPP effectively becomes your landlord and the great thing is that not only does your SIPP not pay tax on the rent you pay it, there is no capital gains tax to pay, as long as you sell the property before you retire. Even if you don't own a business, you might think that owning commercial property as part of your SIPP gives better returns than owning a buy-to-let property.

Opting for a SIPP allows you to move your investments around to benefit from booms in particular markets rather than being fixed to the funds chosen by a traditional pension manager. Every time you move your investments around you will incur transaction charges, but these might be outweighed by the ability to take advantage of stock-market movements that traditional pension funds are too cautious to invest in. Like traditional pensions, you cannot take an income from your SIPP until you are 50 (rising to 55 from 2010).

ISAs

I believe a far better bet for most people is to make use of their ISA allowances. Currently you can invest £7,200 a year into an ISA (made up of cash of £3,600 and the balance in shares, or the whole lot in shares) and you will never pay tax on any gains or dividend payments you make from your ISA; in fact, you don't even have to declare your ISA investments on your tax return. The good thing about this is that it preserves your capital gains tax allowance for other investments, which is currently set at £9,600 a year – great news for anyone who has invested elsewhere, say in property.

If you invested your maximum ISA allowance each year from the age of 40 till you retired at 65 into shares and you achieved the average annual return of 7.2% (which has already been adjusted for inflation), I calculate that you would have built up a pension pot of £468,000. I don't suppose many people will have a spare £7,200 every year, but if you could find £2,000 a year, your pot would still mature to £130,000.

You might take the view that a 7.2% return a year is unrealistic, considering the turmoil in the stock market, in which case you might want to adjust your return to 5% a year, which would turn your £7,200 a year into a final pot of £366,000. However, you might take the view that the current market conditions mean you would be buying in a depressed market which will give you better than average returns. If you thought you might get an average return of 8.5% over 25 years, your pension pot would have nearly £620k in it. Of course, it's possible a future government might change allowances and entitlements to ISAs, but as they replaced the tax-efficient PEPs and TESSAs, the chances are if ISAs are ever withdrawn they will be replaced with a similar savings product.

Based on Barclay's 7.2% figure, I calculate that a 25-year investment in shares would give you a 530% return, i.e. if you put £7,200 in now, in 25 years' time that fund will be worth – in real terms, because that 7.2% already accounts for inflation

– a little over £38,000. Or to put it another way, if you want an annual income of £38,000 a year in 25 years' time, you need to set aside £7,200, or 19% of your target income.

Give some thought to what kind of income you aspire to having in retirement. Look at your budget, see what costs you will still incur and what might fade away in retirement (commuting costs is the obvious expense that disappears). If you work out that you would like an income of £20,000 a year, my figures suggest you need to put away £3,800 a year into an ISA 25 years before you will want the income.

The reason why I advocate ISAs over pensions is their flexibility. You don't have to take one out every year, nor do you have to contribute a fixed amount. You can pay in a lump sum at any point throughout the year or make regular increases throughout the year until you reach the upper limit. But the real beauty of them is that they don't have to be cashed in when you retire. So let's say you start taking ISAs out when you're 40 and you cash in your first ISA at 65, your second ISA when you're 66 and so on. Unlike a pension where the money you put away in your fifties doesn't have time to accrue significant gains before you have to convert it into an annuity, your ISA investments keep on going. In other words, it's not too late to do something about your pension provision.

You would be wise, of course, not just to rely on the market to give you that 7.2% because this figure includes the return achieved by people who manage their investments. If you don't take an active role in choosing and managing your investments, I'd bet that you'll get a lower return.

You decide when you want to take your profits, not the government or the pension company. If you think your ISAs have performed well and you want to take the profits, sell them, and if you think the market still has room for growth, you can hang on to them. And of course you don't have to sell them in the order you took them out. Should one of your ISA funds, or individual share investments, not be producing the returns you had hoped for, you can ditch it and buy another with the money and still keep the tax-free status of that investment –

you can move your ISA funds as much as you like without losing the tax advantages, but you will pay transaction charges.

If you invest into managed funds, ISAs still incur fees – usually 1% or 1.5% of the sum invested – but if you manage your ISA yourself, you will only have the transaction charges (and stamp duty at 0.5%) to pay when you buy your shares, although your self-trade brokerage will probably levy a small annual management fee, perhaps as low as 0.5%.

If you think the ISA option is right for you, you need to do a bit of research into whether or not you think you are capable of investing your ISA allowance yourself. The chances are that you will want help, either from a financial adviser or a fund manager, both of whom will charge for their expertise. However, every spring, the financial press is full of reviews of the best performing funds suitable for ISA investment as the industry encourages people to use up their ISA allowance before the end of the tax year on 5 April. You could scrutinise the reviews and choose your own fund to invest in, and each year you could carry on doing the same thing, selecting funds and fund managers that have good track records and that give you a spread of investments. If you are prepared to put the work in, you save yourself the financial adviser's fee (especially as there's a chance the adviser will only have read the same magazines as you!). You will still pay the fund management fee but this is usually below 1%. In taking this approach, you are committing yourself to conducting an annual review of your finances rather than giving control to someone who cares a lot less about your financial well-being, and I think that's a very smart move.

Property

Many people are relying on the value of their home to provide them with a pension. If they can sell a £500,000 house and downsize into a £250,000 home, they instantly have a quarter of million – tax-free – to invest to provide an income. It's not a bad plan, but what happens if you can't sell your property or it's worth a lot less than you thought? And maybe you really won't want to leave your home and memories behind.

I've already talked about property as an investment, and although you pay capital gains tax on second properties, the tax you eventually pay might be less than you think as you get to deduct all your expenses over the life of the investment and you won't pay CGT on the Annual Exemption Allowance (AEA), currently £9,600 (assuming you haven't used that up elsewhere in your investment portfolio).

Let's say you buy a buy-to-let property when you are 40 for £150,000 with a £50,000 deposit and a £100,000 mortgage. Now let's say it increases in value by a modest 5% a year and you sell it when you are 65 and the mortgage has been paid off. The sale price would be £484,000, which means you've made a capital gain of £334,000. Let's say the purchase, maintenance and sales costs come to £25,000, you can deduct that figure from your gain along with the annual AEA of £9,600, which means you'll pay CGT on £299,400. However, it's actually a better deal for you than that because the taxman calculates your gain from the purchase price. As you only put £50,000 down, you effectively have the value of the mortgage – in this case £100,000 – as a tax-free gain. So although your total gain is actually £434,000, you only pay tax on £299,000 of it. Under current rules, you pay 18% CGT on gains, which means handing over £53,892 to the taxman, or 12.4% of your gain – a *lot* less than you would have paid in income tax if you had earned that money through a salary.

The good thing about having a second property as your pension provision – as opposed to using your own home – is that it doesn't matter quite so much what the property is worth so long as you can still rent it out. It will still provide you with an income until it becomes sensible to sell.

Of course, there is a way to avoid CGT altogether on an investment property, and that's to buy the property you will retire to as your investment. When the time comes, you sell your home – on which no CGT is payable – and move into your investment property.

Alternatives

I appreciate that much of the advice here has not been particularly encouraging for people over 45 who don't have enough earning years left for the compound gains of the market to make a difference, but I would still encourage you to look seriously at ISAs. You might not have enough time to get the returns in time for retiring at 65, but by the time you are 70, the compound returns should have turned your investment into a useful amount of money.

Unless you can really power up your contributions later on in your career, any shares-based investment won't give you much of an income at 65 (and is arguably too risky in terms of market cycles). If you own your own home, you could still think about buying an investment property with some of the equity in your home. Although the mortgage might not be paid off by the time you retire, the mortgage payments will have been reduced in real terms by inflation whereas the rent you receive will have increased. For the first few years of your retirement it will supplement your income and once the mortgage is paid off, it might give you enough to live on.

If that's not an option, it might be that your best course of action is to do nothing. Seriously. Getting to retirement with a modest pot of savings only reduces the amount of state help you will get as much of the income is means-tested. If you have savings above the £6,000 threshold that the authorities let you have, it will reduce what you can claim in pension credits and benefits.

So what should you do if you find yourself with an earnings surge in your fifties and finally able to make some provision for your future? You could try investing in assets – classic cars, fine wines, rare stamps and art are good examples – that you can sell as and when you need the income. The message should be clear now that the younger you start taking your pension provision seriously, the longer you have to benefit from market growth and compound interest. It also means that you can make smaller monthly contributions to whichever pension option you choose to invest in.

 **CHECKLIST**

- ✔ The further you are away from retirement, the less sure you can be that a future government will be able to pay you a liveable pension when you retire.
- ✔ The better provision you make now, the better your income is likely to be in retirement.
- ✔ Traditional pensions are most beneficial if you are either a top-rate taxpayer or if your employer makes contributions.
- ✔ ISAs offer greater flexibility and any income you get from them is tax-free.
- ✔ As a rough guide, you need to invest 19% of the income you would like to live on in retirement 25 years before you'll need it: i.e. if you invest £3,800 this year, it should give you an income of £20,000 in 25 years' time.

PART SIX
The plan

1.
Your personal finance plan

In business, planning is the foundation of growth. At the start of any new venture, I encourage entrepreneurs to write a business plan that maps out what their company does, how it makes money and how it will grow. Over the years, I've become a big fan of business plans because there's something about the act of writing something down that makes it more believable and more attainable. So this final section of the book is about writing your own personal plan so you can plot your financial future, and in doing so, make it more likely that your plans will turn into actions, which will ultimately turn into wealth.

I hope that by the end of this exercise you will have produced a five- to ten-page document to file away. The idea is that you will keep this plan and use it as something to measure your progress against, and as a map to guide you when you get lost in the financial maze. It's very hard to know where you're going without a map, and the plan you're about to write is exactly that – a guide to get you to your financial destination as quickly as possible.

By now you should have a good understanding of the different ways in which you can increase your wealth – you can earn more, save more, invest more and you can spend less on frivolous items. I hope you've also got an idea of what your likely lifetime earning and spending graphs look like and what your financial aspirations are. For this plan, we're going to use everything we've discussed so far to build up a plan that will enable you to amass as much wealth as you can.

Lifetime wealth

Your lifetime wealth differs from your lifetime earnings significantly. While you might stop earning a decent salary in your forties or fifties, the savings and investments you make during your earning years continue to produce returns. The 7.2% return that stock markets have been calculated to give investors means that, compounded over 10 years, it's likely that an invested sum will double in real terms over a decade. Historically, the housing market has given similar returns once inflation has been factored in. That means that if you invest £10,000 at the age of 25, by the time you reach 35 your nest egg should be worth £20,000. By 45 it will have doubled again to £40,000. The sooner you start taking your finances seriously, the longer you have to reap the rewards.

In this plan, I want you to start thinking about your lifetime wealth and how you can balance the five factors of earning, spending, borrowing, saving and investing to maximise your wealth. I don't think it's unreasonable to aspire to double the value of your investments every 10 years so long as you are prepared to take an active involvement in your finances, which is why the structure of this plan is based on what I call Milestone Planning – working out where you want your finances to be on your milestone birthdays of 30, 40, 50 and 60. Your current age will determine where your plan starts, but no matter what age you are, the wealth you accumulate in the very near future can be used to produce bigger returns later on in life.

Here's my estimate of what the lifetime wealth graph of someone who got on the property ladder in their twenties and who works steadily throughout their career might look like:

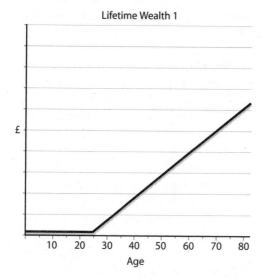

Lifetime Wealth 1

The actual amount of wealth created will depend on the size of the property bought.

Here's the graph for the same person, but this time, as well as benefiting from house-price growth, they also used up their ISA allowance every other year after the age of 30.

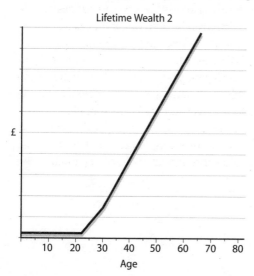

Lifetime Wealth 2

Now, if you thought that was good, let's look at the graph of someone who *creates* wealth.

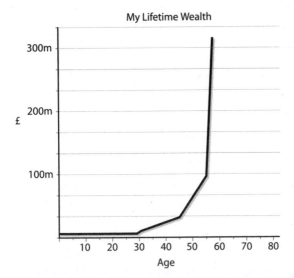

That's actually my lifetime wealth graph and I hope it shows that from a late start with no capital, it's possible for anyone to create wealth and radically change their financial prospects. So what I want you to think about is how you are going to amass wealth over your lifetime. Will it be through property, investments or entrepreneurial flair?

2.
The plan

1. Your net worth

If writing a plan is creating a map for future financial security, you need to know where you're starting from, so in the first section of your plan let's start by working out your current net worth. To do this I want you to make a list of everything you own. Your house, your car, your TV, your CD collection, your clothes, your furniture, your DIY tools, your old Mills & Boon paperbacks, EVERYTHING. Now imagine you sold your whole life on eBay – how much would you get for your possessions? Let's call this figure your Total Assets. But of course, your assets don't tell us how much you're worth – to do that we also need to work out what debts you have.

This might be painful for some people, but if you're going to get to grips with money you have to own up to your debt. If you haven't already done so, gather together your credit card statements, store card statements and bank statements and write down the debts you have – this could be in the form of an overdraft, a bank loan or on a credit card.

Now go back to your list of assets. Were there any items on that list that you had borrowed to buy? Do you have a mortgage on your home? An outstanding loan agreement on your car? A purchase agreement on your sofa or your TV? Add each loan to your list of debts. Let's call this figure your Total Liabilities.

And now for the crucial part. You have to deduct your Liabilities from your Assets to come up with your net worth.

You may think that it would be nice if the figure you've come up with is a big one, or at least one that doesn't start with a minus sign! Of course that would be preferable, but if you have a big mortgage and you're fairly young, there's a very good chance that the total debt on your property easily outstrips the value of your other assets. The key thing here is that a small number isn't a wrong number, and neither is a big number a right one. In fact, the only wrong number to write down at this point is a dishonest one.

If this figure is a decent number, at the very least your personal financial plan should be to double your net worth every decade. If your net worth is minuscule, the work you put into sorting out your finances in the short term will enable you to reap the rewards in the long term.

The next year

Before you write anything else in your plan, get your diary out. Make a note of today's date and make a commitment to yourself that in a year's time you will sit down with your plan and assess your financial progress. So what targets are you going to give yourself for the next year?

You need to decide what your immediate financial priorities are. Depending where you are on your lifetime wealth graph will determine what your choices will be. They might include:

- reducing your level of debt
- boosting your income
- increasing the amount you save
- taking out an ISA or a pension
- starting a business
- buying a property to live in
- buying a property as an investment.

The rest of this section sets out how you are going to achieve your priorities. Write down headings for the five areas of your financial life – earning, spending, borrowing, saving and investing – and think about how you can employ the things you've learnt from reading this book in each of them to make your priorities happen.

In a business plan, the point is to put realistic forecasts on your financial projections, so for each area of your financial life, work out how much you are going to change your financial profile by. So instead of just saying that you're going to reduce your debt, I want you to write down how much you will reduce your debt by. By now, you should know how much money you have to spare each month, or how much you could boost your income by, or what you could sell on eBay, so come up with a reliable figure that you could repay. Is your target to reduce your debt by 50%? Whether the figure you decide on is 10% or 100%, write it down.

The next thing a business plan does is say *how* you are going to achieve your aims, and so should your personal plan. Write down how you are going to clear your debts. Is it through reducing spending, negotiating with your lenders or earning more? What I want you to be able to write is something like this:

I currently owe £12,000 in loans and credit cards. In the next 12 months I calculate that I could reduce my outgoings by £150 a month and I could boost my income by £80. This gives me £230 a month to make increased repayments on my loan. Over 12 months, I will have paid off an additional £2,760 and reduced my overall debt by 23%. When added to my existing repayments, if I continue to overpay, I will be debt-free in three years' time.

Then actually put in the figures in a separate section:

Overall debt   £12,000

Overpayment each month   £280

Reduction in debt in first year   23%

Seeing the figures clearly set out in black and white makes it easier to understand what you're trying to achieve, but you might also want to ask yourself if you could achieve more. If you pushed yourself really hard for a year, could you earn more? Could you halve your debt if you put your mind to it?

You should go into this level of detail for each of your financial aims for the next year. Put a figure on how much you will increase your savings, earnings and investments by, and by how much you will decrease your spending and debts. Then set out *how* you will achieve this, and then ask yourself if your aims are achievable. If they are, ask yourself if you could achieve even more. If you are buying a property, work out how much of a deposit you will need, what the market will be doing for the coming year and investigate the likely mortgage deals on offer so that you can accurately sketch out the financial implications of your purchase.

The more fronts you make changes on, the quicker you will increase your net worth. By the end of this section, you should have a couple of paragraphs on each of the key financial areas setting out your goals for each of them and how you will achieve them.

Your next milestone

Now I want you to start thinking of what you want to have achieved by the time your next milestone birthday comes round. Obviously the further you try to look into the future, the harder it becomes to accurately predict, but with a bit of common sense you can still come up with a reasonable route to financial security.

Maybe you want to give yourself a target of doubling your net worth, or having £25,000 in the bank, or reducing your gearing level from 60% to 30%. Perhaps you'd rather state your goals less clinically and write something along the lines of 'I want to have moved to a bigger house' or 'I want to be running a department at work' or 'I want to have started my own company'.

Once you've come up with your financial goals, you need to look at altering how you employ the five financial factors – earning, spending, borrowing, saving and investing – to achieve your aims. Again, create a heading for each of them and state what steps you will take with each factor to make your dream a reality. If you can plan how you will get to where you want to be, the chances that you will end up there increase dramatically.

Think about your levels of investment and debt: are you sure that you are moving out of the red and towards a surplus? Write down what you think your level of debt should be at your next milestone. And if you've started to amass some wealth, how are you going to use that wealth to benefit from the long-term gains that investments traditionally offer? Are you hoping your current investments will mature by the next milestone, or the one after that, or the one after that? For each investment you have, write down what you're hoping it will deliver, and when.

The next thing to look at is your earnings curve. If your next milestone coincides with a period when you are likely to earn more, make a plan for what you will do with the excess – will you pay off the mortgage, buy a second property, increase investment levels? And if you're about to go through a period of lower earnings, how will you need to adjust your standard of living to cope?

And the milestone after that?

Now spend a bit of time thinking about how – in an ideal world – you might spend your future. When you envisage yourself at 40, 50, 60 and beyond, what kind of lifestyle do you aspire to have? Think about how you will be earning an income and where you will be living. Write down a few lines about how you would like your life to progress. Does your vision follow on from your aspirations from the previous milestone? Ask yourself if your ambitions seem plausible given your income levels. If they're not, what are you going to do about it? Might you need to change careers or think of a way of creating wealth? A couple of hours now spent writing a few paragraphs will help you make choices that will steer you towards your goal.

In terms of increasing your net wealth, what do you think will be achievable given the likely pattern of your future earnings and investments? Is a doubling every 10 years doable? Can you exceed that rate of growth somehow? What can you do to speed up the rate at which you increase your wealth?

For each of your remaining milestones, give some thought to the kinds of choices you will have to make to be able to live your dream life. Now ask yourself what you have to do in the short term to make your long-term ambitions a reality and, if necessary, go back and amend your commitments for the next year.

Retirement

Before you finish your plan, give some thought as to how you are going to fund your retirement. Think about whether your earning patterns make taking out a traditional pension a sensible option or if you need to make alternative arrangements. What percentage of your current income should you be setting aside to have a decent income in the future? What investments can you make now that will give you the rewards when you are older? Write a few lines that set out how you will fund your old age, and if you aren't sure, put it in your plan that by this time next year you will have formulated a retirement strategy.

Annual review

This is actually the most important bit. I want you to make a commitment to go through this process every year by getting last year's plan out and measuring how you've done against your goals. Did everything go to plan? If you weren't able to achieve your aims, can you identify why? And if you exceeded them, what can you learn from your success? Celebrate your successes but if you fell short, make sure you understand why.

Each year you should set your annual goals and review your long-term plans. I imagine your ambitions will change as you age, and your short-term goals will be guided by the wider economic cycle as well as your personal financial cycle.

Each year, ask yourself what your priorities are and, crucially, what the opportunities are. What's going on in the world that can impact – positively or negatively – on your finances? In economic cycles there are good times to save, chances to earn over the odds, bad times to invest and the right time to sell. Each year, assess where you are in your personal cycle and the broader economic cycle and spot the opportunities and pitfalls ahead of you. Work out what your next career move ought to be and check that you will be in a position to get the right job when it comes along.

As part of this annual review, you should also look at any financial products you have and ask yourself if your savings and investments are working hard enough and if you are using any debt efficiently. Go and talk to some financial advisers, read the papers and watch the Budget. The more you stay informed, the more likely it is that you will prosper.

Once you've updated your personal plan, put it somewhere safe so that you can use it like a map to guide you through tough decisions. If you ever have trouble making a financial choice, take out your plan and read it. Reconnect with your ambitions for your life and work out if the dilemma in question takes you towards or away from your goals. By setting out your finances in black and white, it should take the mystery out of money and put you in control. I promise you that the more responsibility you take for your finances, the better off you will be.

A template for your plan

1.
Your net worth

Assets	£
Liabilities	£
Net worth	£

	Earning*	Spending	Borrowing	Saving	Investing
2. **The next year** Financial priority					
3. **Your next milestone** Aims + ambitions					
4. **Subsequent milestones** Aims + ambitions					

* Increase earnings by x % by doing a, b and c.*

5.
Retirement
Aims + ambitions

Outline how these will be funded

Glossary

AER

Stands for Annual Equivalent Rate and is the rate of interest paid on savings. It's usually higher than the actual interest rate because it takes into account the effects of compound interest over a year.

AIM

Stands for the Alternative Investment Market where shares in smaller and newer companies are traded. AIM investments are seen as riskier than those in the main Stock Exchange, but with the potential for bigger rewards.

Annual Return

This has two meanings. The first refers to the financial return you get on your investment in a year, and the second refers to the accounts limited companies must submit to Companies House each year.

Annuity

The annual payment made by an insurance company in exchange for a lump sum. You are legally required to buy an annuity with 75% of your pension fund.

APR

Annual Percentage Rate. This is the rate at which loans are advertised to allow comparison between products. A monthly interest rate of 1.5% works out at an APR of 19.56%.

Bonds

Bonds are a financial product that allow companies (and governments) to raise money without giving away equity. Customers buy bonds in return for guaranteed interest payments and the return of their initial investment at an agreed future date. Bonds have two advantages over other investments – a guaranteed income and a guarantee that the investment will be returned (unless the company goes into administration). However, there is a chance that the original investment will not keep pace with inflation. You do not have to hold the bond until the end of the agreement and can trade it, which may mean you may get a higher price than you paid for it.

Buy-to-let

The buying of property to let out to tenants instead of using it as a primary home.

Capital gains tax (CGT)

The tax paid on any increases in the value of assets when they are sold. There is currently a flat rate of 18% payable on any gains above the tax-free threshold of £9,600 a year. The exception for this is the Entrepreneur's Relief on the disposal of business assets, on which 10% is paid on the first million (this is a lifetime allowance).

Collateral

The security asked for by banks when issuing a loan. So if you borrow to start a business, they might ask for your home as collateral.

Deflation

The opposite of inflation. It is the downward price movement of goods and services. So if goods that cost £100 last year cost £95 this year, the rate of deflation would be 5%.

Dividend

A payment made by a company to its shareholders. Dividends usually increase in line with the profits a company makes. Dividend payments are at the discretion of the company's board and are not mandatory.

Equity

In property, the equity in a building is the value of the property minus the mortgage debt that is outstanding.

Funds

Most firms of stockbrokers offer managed funds to investors. Customers buy shares in the fund which in turn buys shares in individual companies. This spreads the risk of stock-market investment, and shares are traded according to market conditions without customers having an active say in those trades.

Gearing

Usually expressed as a percentage, a company's or individual's gearing is their relationship of debt to equity. If you borrow £5 million to buy a company worth £10 million, your gearing is 50%. The lower the gearing level, the less risk there is to the lender, and the less vulnerable the company (or individual) is to rises in the cost of borrowing.

Gilts

Gilts, or gilt-edged bonds, are bonds issued by the government. Like other bonds, they are tradable and their prices usually decrease when interest rates and inflation rise. Low interest rates and low inflation make them more valuable. Income from gilts is taxable, but the capital gain is tax-free.

Gross

The amount paid before tax is deducted.

In the black

In credit, making a profit or solvent.

In the red

Someone who's 'in the red' is in debt. It's an accountancy term as negative numbers are often shown in red in spreadsheets, rather than black. Rather worryingly, a survey by financial advisers Sesame found out that 12% of teenagers thought being in the red meant being embarrassed!

IFA

Independent Financial Adviser. You can find a local one at unbiased.co.uk.

Inflation

The opposite of deflation, inflation is the upward price movement of goods and services, usually expressed as an annual percentage.

Interest rates

The percentage banks pay to savers on their deposits or charge borrowers on their loans. Usually savers get lower rates than borrowers. If you're saving, you want to find the highest interest rate, and if you're borrowing, you want to find the lowest. Example: if you save £10,000 in an account paying 5% interest, at the end of a full year, you will have a balance of £10,500 before tax is deducted.

NB. The Bank of England sets the national interest rates, but that headline figure probably won't be what your bank charges you on your loans or pays you on your savings. Typically, commercial banks lend at slightly above the national rate, and pay at slightly below it.**ISA**
Individual Savings Account that lets you invest up to £7,200 (of which £3,600 can be in cash) tax-free.

Leveraging

Another word for gearing or borrowing to invest. With a loan you can 'leverage' your own cash to produce higher returns.

Liability

Sometimes used to describe debts, but may refer to an asset or investment that is likely to decrease in value.

LIBOR

The London Interbank Offered Rate. This is the rate that banks lend money to each other. In good times it tends to be just a per cent or two above the Bank of England rate, and the higher above the BoE rate it is, the more cautious the market is and the more expensive borrowing becomes for banks' customers.

Liquid asset

Either cash or an asset that can be traded or turned into cash easily.

Negative equity

When the value of an asset is worth less than the loan taken out to buy the asset, usually property.

Net

The amount paid after tax and NICs have been deducted.

NICs

National Insurance Contributions (NICs) are deducted from earnings in addition to income tax. The exact amount differs for employed and self-employed workers and whether your contributions are paid into a pension. Most employees pay 11% of their earnings between £105 and £770 a week, and 1% on everything above that.

Principal

The original amount lent to a borrower before interest is added. If, for example, you have an interest-only mortgage, it means you are only paying the interest on the principal, not the principal itself which would still be outstanding at the end of the mortgage term.

Recession

A period in the economic cycle when the economy is contracting rather than expanding. Typically companies experience falling profits but static costs, which leads to redundancies and closures.

ROCE

Return on Capital Employed. This differs from ROI because instead of investing your own money, you might have borrowed to invest. If you put up £25 and borrow £75 (on which you pay £5 interest) to invest £100 and get a return of £125, your net return is £20, giving you an 80% ROCE on the £25 you invested.

ROI

Return on Investment. If you invest £100 into something and get £125 back, you have an ROI of 25%.

Secured loans

A loan secured against an asset, typically your home, which can be seized if you fail to repay the loan.

Spread

The difference between the buying and selling price of stocks and currencies.

Stagflation

The dreaded combination of inflation and stagnation where the economy is not growing but prices continue to rise.

Tax

The amount paid to the government from earnings to pay for services. There are many kinds of taxes, but the one that has the biggest impact on most people is income tax. Current income tax rates are 20% on earnings between £6,035 and £40,835 and 40% on earnings above that level. Earnings below £6,035 are tax-free.

Tax credits

Payments made by the government to workers on low incomes, especially parents paying for childcare. A single, childless worker can get help in the form of tax credits if their income is below £12,800 a year, and parents who pay for childcare are entitled to help if their household income is below £58,000 a year.

Unsecured loans

A loan offered without asking for a charge on your assets. Typically, unsecured loans incur a slightly higher interest rate than secured loans.

VAT

Value Added Tax. A tax added to most goods and services (although many items considered essential, like food and books, are exempt) and the standard rate is typically 17.5%. This amount was temporarily reduced on 1 December 2008 to 15% for 13 months. Some goods and services incur a lower rate of VAT. Companies and sole traders with a turnover in excess of £67,000 are obliged to register for VAT which can be a help with cashflow. Many small businesses find they are better off if they register.

Index